Information Security Risk Management
for
ISO 27001 / ISO 27002

Information Security Risk Management for ISO 27001 / ISO 27002

Third edition

ALAN CALDER

STEVE G WATKINS

IT Governance Publishing

Every possible effort has been made to ensure that the information contained in this book is accurate at the time of going to press, and the publisher and the author cannot accept responsibility for any errors or omissions, however caused. Any opinions expressed in this book are those of the author, not the publisher. Websites identified are for reference only, not endorsement, and any website visits are at the reader's own risk. No responsibility for loss or damage occasioned to any person acting, or refraining from action, as a result of the material in this publication can be accepted by the publisher or the author.

Apart from any fair dealing for the purposes of research or private study, or criticism or review, as permitted under the Copyright, Designs and Patents Act 1988, this publication may only be reproduced, stored or transmitted, in any form, or by any means, with the prior permission in writing of the publisher or, in the case of reprographic reproduction, in accordance with the terms of licences issued by the Copyright Licensing Agency. Enquiries concerning reproduction outside those terms should be sent to the publisher at the following address:

IT Governance Publishing Ltd
Unit 3, Clive Court
Bartholomew's Walk
Cambridgeshire Business Park
Ely, Cambridgeshire
CB7 4EA
United Kingdom
www.itgovernancepublishing.co.uk

First published in the United Kingdom in 2007 (as *Information Security Risk Management for ISO27001 / ISO17799*) by IT Governance Publishing.

Second edition published in the United Kingdom in 2010 by IT Governance Publishing
ISBN 978-1-84928-043-3

Third edition published in the United Kingdom in 2019 by IT Governance Publishing
ISBN: 978-1-78778-136-8

ABOUT THE AUTHORS

Alan Calder founded IT Governance Limited in 2002 and began working full time for the company in 2007. He is now Group CEO of GRC International Group plc, the AIM-listed company that owns IT Governance Ltd. Prior to this, Alan had a number of roles including CEO of Business Link London City Partners from 1995 to 1998 (a government agency focused on helping growing businesses to develop), CEO of Focus Central London from 1998 to 2001 (a training and enterprise council), CEO of Wide Learning from 2001 to 2003 (a supplier of e-learning) and the Outsourced Training Company (2005). Alan was also chairman of CEME (a public private sector skills partnership) from 2006 to 2011.

Alan is an acknowledged international cyber security guru and a leading author on information security and IT governance issues. He has been involved in the development of a wide range of information security management training courses that have been accredited by the International Board for IT Governance Qualifications (IBITGQ). Alan has consulted for clients in the UK and abroad, and is a regular media commentator and speaker.

Steve G Watkins is an executive director at GRC International Group plc. He is a contracted technical assessor for UKAS – advising on its assessments of certification bodies offering ISMS/ISO 27001 and ITSMS/ISO 20000-1 accredited certification and also undertakes information security assessments of forensic science laboratories seeking accreditation to the Forensic Science Regulator's codes of practice and conduct.

He is a member of ISO/IEC JTC 1/SC 27, the international technical committee responsible for information security, cyber security and privacy standards, and chairs the UK National Standards Body's technical committee IST/33 (information security, cyber security and privacy protection) that mirrors it. Steve is also involved with technical committees: RM/1 (risk management) and RM/1/-/3 (responsible for BS 31111, providing guidance for boards and senior management on cyber risk and resilience); IST/060/02 (IT service management) and IDT/001/0-/04 (data protection).

Steve was an active member of IST/33/-/6, which developed BS 7799-3.

Alan Calder and Steve G Watkins have written a number of other books together, including *IT Governance: An International Guide to Data Security and ISO 27001/ISO 27002* (seventh edition published by Kogan Page, 2019).

A list of all their publications can be found at the back of this book.

CONTENTS

Contents

Contents

INTRODUCTION

In today's information economy, the development, exploitation and protection of information and associated assets are key to the long-term competitiveness and survival of corporations and entire economies. The protection of information and associated assets – information security – is therefore overtaking physical asset protection as a fundamental corporate governance responsibility. An information security management system (ISMS) that provides "a systematic approach for establishing, implementing, operating, monitoring, reviewing, maintaining and improving an organization's information security to achieve business objectives"[1] has become a critical corporate discipline, alongside marketing, sales, HR and financial management.

A key corporate governance objective is to ensure that the organisation has an appropriate balance of risk and reward in its business operations and, as a consequence, enterprise risk management (ERM) increasingly provides a framework within which organisations can assess and manage risks in their business plan. The recognition of substantial, strategic risk in information and communication technologies has led to the development of IT governance.[2]

The changing global economy, together with recent corporate and IT governance developments, all provide the

---

[1] ISO/IEC 27000:2018, Clause 4.2.1 'Overview and principles'.

[2] Other books by the same authors discuss these issues in greater detail. See, for instance, *IT Governance: An International Guide to Data Security and ISO27001/ISO27002*, (Kogan Page, 2019).

context within which organisations have to assess risks to the information assets on which their organisations, and the delivery of their business plan objectives, depend. Information security management decisions are entirely driven by specific decisions made as an outcome of a risk assessment process in relation to identified risks and specific information assets.

Risk assessment is, therefore, the core competence of information security management.

The Introduction (Clause 0) of ISO/IEC 27002:2013 (ISO 27002), the international code of best practice for ISMSs, supports this business- and risk-oriented approach: "Resources employed in implementing controls need to be balanced against the business harm likely to result from security issues in the absence of those controls. The results of a risk assessment will help guide and determine the appropriate management action and priorities for managing information security risks and for implementing controls selected to protect against these risks."[3]

A growing number of organisations are adopting this approach to the management of risk. A number of national or proprietary standards that deal with information security risk management have emerged over the years. They all have much in common. ISO 27001 is the international standard that sets out the requirements for an ISMS and provides an approach to risk management consistent with all other guidance; indeed many of the other frameworks that are available are based on ISO 27001. This approach is also

---

[3] ISO/IEC 27002:2013, Clause 0.2 'Information security requirements'.

appropriate for organisations complying with the Payment Card Industry Data Security Standard (PCI DSS), and supports compliance with other legal and regulatory requirements, such as the EU's General Data Protection Regulation (GDPR) and Directive on security of network and information systems (NIS Directive).

Of course, every organisation needs to determine its criteria for accepting risks, and identify the levels of risk it will accept. It is a truism to point out that there is a relationship between the levels of risk and reward in any business. Most businesses, particularly those subject to the Sarbanes-Oxley Act of 2002 and, in the UK, the FRC's *Guidance on Risk Management, Internal Control and Related Financial and Business Reporting* and the UK Corporate Governance Code, will want to be very clear about which risks they will accept and which they won't, the extent to which they will accept risks and how they wish to control them. Management needs to specify its approach, in general and in particular, so that the business can be managed within that context. As we have indicated, risk assessment, as an activity, should be approached within the context of the organisation's broader ERM framework.

All too often, organisations enter into risk management without considering that the practice must be part of something larger. A risk assessment is not an end in itself: a risk assessment must provide outputs that are useful to the organisation. The goal of a risk assessment methodology must be to effect the organisation's ISMS.

While ISO 27002 is a code of practice, ISO/IEC 27001:2013 (ISO 27001) is a specification that sets out the requirements for an ISMS. ISO 27001 is explicit in requiring that an information security risk assessment is used to inform the selection of controls.[4] Risk assessment, as we've said, is therefore the core competence of information security management.

Organisations that design and implement an ISMS in line with ISO 27001 can have it assessed by a third-party certification body and if, after audit, it is found to be in line with ISO 27001, an accredited certificate of conformity can be issued.[5]

This standard is increasingly seen as offering a practical solution to the growing range of information-related regulatory requirements, as well as helping organisations to more cost-effectively counter the increasingly sophisticated and varied range of information security threats in the modern information economy.[6] As a result, a rapidly growing number of companies around the world are seeking certification to ISO 27001, providing a means of demonstrating to clients and other stakeholders their commitment and intent with regard to information security.

An ISMS developed and based on risk acceptance criteria, and using third-party accredited certification to provide an independent verification of the level of assurance, is an extremely useful management tool. Such an ISMS offers the

---

[4] A 'control' is a measure that modifies a risk. See ISO 27000:2018, Clause 2.16.

[5] There is a full description of the process of accredited certification in *IT Governance: An International Guide to Data Security and ISO27001/ISO27002* by Alan Calder and Steve Watkins (Kogan Page, 2019).

[6] See *The Case for ISO 27001:2013* by Alan Calder (ITGP, 2013) for detailed coverage of the business, contractual and regulatory reasons that should lead an organisation to consider developing an ISMS in line with ISO 27001.

opportunity to define and monitor service levels internally, as well as in contractor/partner organisations, thus demonstrating the extent to which there is effective control of those risks for which directors and senior management are accountable.

It is becoming increasingly common for ISO 27001 certification to be a prerequisite in service specification procurement documents and, as buyers become more sophisticated in their understanding of the ISO 27001 accredited certification scheme, so they will increasingly set out their requirements more specifically, not only in terms of certification itself but also in respect to the scope of the certification and the level of assurance they require. This rapid maturing in the understanding of buyers is driving organisations to improve the quality of their ISMS.

The level of assurance relates, of course, directly to the risk assessment and management aspects of creating and maintaining an ISO 27001-compliant ISMS. It is this key aspect that ensures that a consistent level of assurance is achieved across all facets of information security within an organisation.

ISO 27001 is a specification for an ISMS. As we have said, it is based on risk assessment, both initially and on an ongoing basis. ISO 27001 goes so far as to specify the requirements that an information security risk management approach must satisfy. While there are many recognised – and valid – approaches to risk assessment, an organisation that wishes to achieve ISO 27001 certification must meet the requirements set out in the Standard itself. There is no room for half measures: either a risk assessment methodology is in line with the requirements of ISO 27001, in which case accredited certification is within reach, or it is not, in which case accredited certification is not achievable.

This book has been written to expand on guidance that is already contained within other ISO 27001 implementation books by the same authors. It draws on emerging national and international best practice around risk assessment, including the British Standard BS 7799-3:2017 (BS 7799-3), which was published to align with the 2013 version of ISO 27001. It has also been written to provide detailed and practical guidance to information security and risk management teams on how to develop and implement a risk assessment and risk management process that will be in line with the requirements of ISO 27001, that will reflect the best-practice guidance of BS 7799-3, and which will simultaneously deliver real, bottom-line business benefits.

CHAPTER 1: RISK MANAGEMENT

"Risk", says NIST,[7] is the "measure of the extent to which an entity is threatened by a potential circumstance or event, and is typically a function of: (i) the adverse impact that would arise if the circumstance or event occurs; and (ii) the likelihood of occurrence."[8] ISO/IEC 27000:2018 *Information security management systems – Overview and vocabulary* (ISO 27000) defines risk as the "effect of uncertainty on objectives", with a subsidiary note stating that "Risk is often expressed in terms of a combination of the consequences of an event (including changes in circumstances) and the associated likelihood of occurrence".

The NIST definition of risk is in line with that used in ISO 27000, and is the first indicator that a risk assessment that will meet the requirements of ISO 27001 will also be in line with the NIST recommendations. The main difference between the NIST and ISO 27000 definitions is that the latter encompasses the possibility of risks having positive consequences.

ISO 27000 has a further note, however, that "Information security risk is associated with the potential that threats will exploit vulnerabilities of an information asset or group of information assets and thereby cause harm to an organization", which retains the focus on risks to information assets reflected in previous versions of the ISO 27000 family

---

[7] The National Institute of Standards and Technology is the US federal agency that develops and promotes measurement, standards and technology.
[8] NIST SP 800-30.

of standards, while also encompassing an approach that focuses on scenarios that could occur and cause harm.

BS 7799-3 refers to ISO 27000 for its definitions and its guidance is given on this basis.

All organisations face risks of one sort or another on a daily basis and ISO 27001 expects that an organisation's information security management policy will align with "the strategic direction of the organization"[9] and that it will be "appropriate to the purpose of the organization".[10] It is therefore appropriate to consider, briefly, the organisational risk management context.

Risk management: two phases

Risk management is the process that allows managers to balance the operational and economic costs of protective measures and achieve gains in mission capability by protecting the IT systems and data that support their organisation's missions.[11]

Organisations develop and implement risk management strategies in order to reduce negative impacts and to provide a structured, consistent basis for making decisions around risk mitigation options. For the purpose of considering the topic of risk management, it has two phases: risk assessment and risk treatment, but in practice it is a continual activity that includes horizon scanning, risk assessment, risk decisions, risk treatment(s), communication, reassessment, further treatments, and so on.

---

[9] ISO 27001, Clause 5.1 a).
[10] ISO 27001, Clause 5.2 a).
[11] NIST SP 800-30, Introduction.

Risk assessment is the process of identifying and estimating the risks that the organisation may be subject to.

Risk treatment is the process of responding to identified risks in light of risk decisions.

Risk assessment typically adopts one of two methods:

- The process of identifying scenarios, their impact on the organisation and the frequency at which they may occur.

- Focusing on information assets and the threats that they are subject to. Considering the vulnerabilities the threats might exploit enables the risk assessor to identify the likelihood and impact of each identified risk.

In the simplified two-step explanation of risk management, the risk assessment phase then leads into the risk treatment phase. Any decisions and/or actions taken in light of the risk assessment are taken outside the risk assessment process, and are part of the risk treatment planning activity that, together with the risk assessment process, is the other constituent of *risk management*. Risk management is the superset of, and therefore includes, risk assessment.

Risk assessment and risk treatment are the two sub-processes of risk management, as seen in relation to an asset-based assessment in Figure 1.

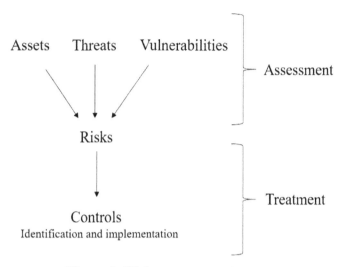

Figure 1: Risk management

While it is true to say that the risk management process starts with a risk assessment, it is helpful to have a broader understanding of the overall environment in which most risk management activity takes place.

Risk management, as we have said, includes both risk assessment and risk treatment, and is a discipline that deals with the effect of uncertainty. While uncertainty will ordinarily take the form of negative impacts, it is possible that positive impacts might also be identified and pursued. Most risk assessments are more interested in non-speculative risks (risks from which only a loss can occur) than in speculative risks (risks from which either a profit or loss could occur) except insofar that a speculative risk can mitigate the negatives. Speculative risk is more frequently the topic of the organisation's business strategy.

Risk management plans usually have four focuses for how each risk is to be addressed. These are to:

1. Avoid/reject the risk by deciding not to pursue the practices and/or arrangements that give rise to it;

2. Retain/take the risk, keeping it under review;

3. Modify/reduce risks to 'acceptable' levels through the application of controls; and/or

4. Share the risk with another party, whether through contract or insurance.

The following diagram illustrates the concept of 'controlling' risk. The greater the likelihood, or the more negative the impact, the greater the risk.

Controls, or risk mitigation, should be designed to reduce likelihood and/or impact such that the magnitude of the risk is reduced below a tolerance threshold. This tolerance threshold is also often known as the risk acceptance level or risk appetite.

Risk treatment plans reduce identified risks to the agreed risk acceptance level, represented by the shaded area in Figure 2.

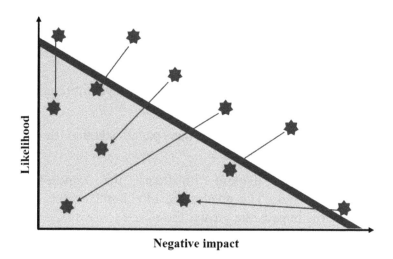

Figure 2: Risk treatment

Pure, permanent risks are usually identifiable in economic terms; they have a financially measurable potential impact on the organisation's assets. Risk management strategies are usually, therefore, based on an assessment of the economic benefits that the organisation can derive from an investment in a particular control or combination of controls. In other words, for every control that the organisation might implement, the calculation would be that the cost of implementation would be outweighed, preferably significantly, by the economic benefits that derive from, or economic losses that are avoided as a result of, its implementation.

The organisation should define its criteria for accepting risks (for example, it might say that it will accept any risk whose economic impact is less than the cost of controlling it) and for controlling risks (for example, it might say that any risk that has both a high likelihood and a high impact must be controlled to an identified level, or threshold). The ERM framework is, most usually, the framework within which organisations define their risk acceptance criteria in the light of their risk appetite and, as a result of which, define their systems of internal control. It often sets the parameters for discipline-specific risk considerations such as information security.

Enterprise risk management

ERM is an increasingly important component of corporate governance and it provides an overall context for internal control activities.

Guidance on Risk Management, Internal Control and Related Financial and Business Reporting

The FRC's *Guidance on Risk Management*[12] is very clear on the steps that UK-listed companies should take in respect of risk: paragraph 28 states that:

> The risk management and internal control systems encompass the policies, culture, organisation, behaviours, processes, systems and other aspects of a company that, taken together:
>
> facilitate its effective and efficient operation by enabling it to assess current and emerging risks, respond appropriately to risks and significant control failures and to safeguard its assets;
>
> help to reduce the likelihood and impact of poor judgement in decision-making; risk-taking that exceeds

---

[12] The *Guidance on Risk Management* is available for download from the Financial Reporting Council's website: *www.frc.org.uk*.

the levels agreed by the board; human error; or control processes being deliberately circumvented;

help ensure the quality of internal and external reporting; and

help ensure compliance with applicable laws and regulations, and also with internal policies with respect to the conduct of business.

Paragraph 29 recognises that "A company's systems of risk management and internal control will include [...] information and communication systems". Paragraph 37 is clear that "Effective controls [...] cover many aspects of a business, including strategic, financial, operational and compliance".

Basel 2

Pillar 1 of the Basel 2 Accord aims to align a bank's minimum capital requirements more closely to its actual risk of economic loss, aiming to establish an explicit capital charge for a "bank's exposures to the risk of losses caused by failures in systems, processes, or staff or that are caused by external events".[13] Those banks that take an approach to measuring, managing and controlling their operational risk exposures appropriate to the risk area will have lower capital requirements.

---

[13] BIS press release, 26 June 2004.

COSO

A widely respected ERM framework is the one developed by COSO,[14] the body that was also responsible for developing the internal control framework that has been used in the vast majority of organisations to demonstrate compliance with the Sarbanes-Oxley Act of 2002. The COSO *ERM – Integrated Framework* is in line with both *Guidance on Risk Management* and Basel 2 when it defines ERM as:

> a process, effected by an entity's board of directors, management and other personnel, applied in strategy setting and across the enterprise, designed to identify potential events that may affect the entity, and manage risk to be within its risk appetite, to provide reasonable assurance regarding the achievement of entity objectives.

This definition contains many of the attributes that are also relevant to information security risk management. ERM objectives include:

- Aligning risk appetite and strategy;

- Consistently applying risk treatment criteria (enhancing risk response decisions), with the options to: accept, reject, transfer, control;

- Reducing operational surprises and losses;

- Identifying and managing multiple and cross-enterprise risks;

---

[14] The Committee of Sponsoring Organizations of the Treadway Commission (*www.coso.org*).

- Seizing opportunities – after considering a full range of potential events; and

- Enabling risk-related deployment of capital.

Organisations that already have an ERM framework of some description in place are at an advantage in taking forward the ISO 27001 risk management process, which should be slotted seamlessly within that overarching corporate ERM framework. The ERM objectives and risk acceptance criteria should be carried through into the ISO 27001 risk management process, which should contribute to providing the board and management with a greater depth and breadth of assurance that information risk is being managed within pre-approved guidelines.

A pre-existing ERM is not, though, a prerequisite for the successful development and implementation of an ISO 27001-conforming ISMS. Organisations that do not already have in place such a framework will need, at the very least, to develop their approach to risk sufficiently to be able to ensure that their information security risk assessment is business-driven, and is structured, systematic and reproducible. Moreover, the risk assessment approach will have to take into account the organisation's "legal and regulatory requirements and contractual obligations".[15]

It is also not necessary to wait until the organisation develops a strategic approach to risk, or even an ERM framework. Information security management needs to be tackled more urgently than the timeframe that the development of an ERM framework will usually allow.

---

[15] ISO 27001, Clause 4.2, note.

1: Risk management

There are always issues of integration that have to be addressed when an ISO 27001-conforming risk assessment methodology is being developed within or alongside a broader, more strategic approach to risk management. For instance, definitions, roles and responsibilities could all be different, timeframes could be seriously out of alignment, and the ERM framework quite often tackles risk on a top-down basis, while many organisations adopt a bottom-up approach to the identification and control of risk to satisfy ISO 27001.

CHAPTER 2: RISK ASSESSMENT METHODOLOGIES

In this book we use the terms 'method' and 'methodology' interchangeably. A method is (as most standard dictionaries explain) simply a 'way of doing something'. A method, in other words, will contain principles and procedures, describing both what must be done and how it must be done. A risk assessment methodology, therefore, is a description of the principles and procedures (preferably documented) that describe how information security risks should be assessed and evaluated.

An effective, defined, ISO 27001-conforming information security risk assessment methodology should provide the organisation (particularly its board and management) with an assurance that all the relevant risks have been factored into the process, and that there is a commonly defined and understood means of communicating and acting on the results of that risk assessment. This does, of course, also mean that there will be a wider and better understanding, across the organisation, of the risks that are being dealt with, and of the practical business support budget that will be needed to implement the required controls.

We recognise that there are many established risk assessment methodologies. However, as we said earlier, an ISO 27001 risk assessment has to contain, as a minimum, a specific set of steps and some currently recognised methodologies simply do not meet the requirements of ISO 27001. This is because they do not contain the required steps, or because they do not include the criteria for performing information security risk assessments and acceptance criteria, or even because they provide a primarily technology-focused information security risk assessment. We are not going to address those methodologies here.

Publicly available risk assessment standards

There are three primary information security risk management standards that we are interested in related to ISO 27001. The key standards that we refer to here are:

ISO 27005 (*Information technology – Security techniques – Information security risk management*) is the international standard for information security risk management. This has recently been updated and reissued as ISO/IEC 27005:2018, bringing it into line with the amended requirements (and possibilities) of ISO 27001:2013.

BS 7799-3:2017[16] (*Information security management systems – Part 3: Guidelines for information security risk management*) has been published in the UK as guidance on the subject, and is totally aligned with ISO 27001:2013 and other more recent relevant standards.

NIST SP 800-30 (*Guide for Conducting Risk Assessments*) was published in September 2012 and is still current. Like ISO 27005 and BS 7799-3, it provides guidance and is not a specification. This guidance is consistent with, but does not totally fulfil, the requirements of ISO 27001 and we have,

---

[16] In the UK, ISO/IEC 27001 was previously dual-numbered as BS 7799-2, and ISO/IEC 27002 was dual-numbered as BS 7799-1 (they were exactly the same standards, with alternative document numbering). BS 7799-3 therefore fitted neatly into that numbering sequence, with the original version being published in 2006. It was later withdrawn, leaving ISO 27005 as the single source of guidance in the ISMS-related standards family.

therefore, drawn on the NIST document wherever it provides useful guidance.

BS 7799-3 identifies the context in which organisations seek to manage their risks: "Organizations have objectives, and in exploiting the opportunities that they create or seize to meet those objectives, they can encounter risks which need to be managed for the objectives to be fully realized. Some of those risks are information security risks".[17]

Clause 6.1.2 of ISO 27001 sets the requirements for risk assessments. The steps in the information security risk assessment process are, as we shall see, to:

1. Establish the information security risk criteria, consisting of both the requirements that trigger the need for an information security risk assessment to be conducted, and the risk acceptance criteria;

2. Identify the information security risks;

3. Analyse the information security risks; and

4. Evaluate the information security risks.

This process must be able to ensure that repeated risk assessments produce consistent, valid and comparable results. It is important to note that these steps apply to the information security risk assessment, but ISO 27001 also specifies that the organisation needs to assess the risks to the management system itself, including the risk of the ISMS not achieving its intended outcomes.

Clause 6.1.1 of the Standard describes how risk assessments should fit into the broader ISMS. Remember that a risk

---

[17] BS 7799-3, Clause 4.

assessment is not an end in itself: an ISO 27001 risk assessment should not only help the organisation protect its information and related assets but also do so as part of the larger ISMS, which should serve the organisation's strategic interests and objectives.

While the risk assessment steps are mandatory, there are, broadly speaking, two approaches that can be adopted: asset-based and scenario-based. Beyond that, we will also still have to define a methodology for assessing risk and, for help in that, we will turn again to BS 7799-3 and ISO 27005.

BS 7799-3 and ISO 27005 provide substantial guidance on information security risk assessment, but no prescriptive guidance on which method is preferable because every organisation is encouraged to choose the most applicable approach for its industry, complexity and risk environment.

BS 7799-3 identifies two possible approaches to risk identification and analysis, and recognises that it is possible to blend these together:

Scenario-based assessments, in which risks are identified and assessed by considering events and their consequences. The organisation estimates the likelihood of the event occurring and the severity of its consequences in order to determine the level of risk.

Asset-threat-vulnerability assessments, in which risk identification and analysis take into account the value of assets associated with information (and the information assets themselves), the threats that apply to each asset and the vulnerabilities that the threats could exploit.

In relative terms, the first of these is likely to be more valuable from a high-level perspective, and the second is naturally more granular and detailed. Either approach can

2: Risk assessment methodologies

work for an ISO 27001 ISMS; the critical thing is to think through the strategic implications of each methodology, and the relative benefits and drawbacks of each.

ISO 27001, ISO 27002, ISO 27005 and BS 7799-3 reference ISO 27000 for the definitions of risk, risk analysis, risk assessment, risk evaluation, risk management and risk treatment. We recommend that these definitions are, for the sake of consistency, adopted by any organisation tackling risk management and, as indicated at the outset, this book will proceed on that basis.

In any case, it is clear that information security risk assessment is a systematic examination of the probability and consequences of risks or, in our terms, the systematic and methodical consideration of:

a) The business harm likely to result from a range of business failures; and

b) The realistic likelihood of such failures occurring.

The information security risk assessment must be a formal process. In other words, the process must be planned and the input data, its analysis and the results should all be recorded. 'Formal' does not mean that risk assessment tools must be used, but in most situations they will improve the process and add significant value; in many organisations, it will not be possible to carry out a risk assessment without using an appropriate tool. (We provide information on risk assessment tools later in this book.) The complexity of the risk assessment will depend on the complexity of the organisation and of the risks under review, and in particular, approaches to grouping assets or assessing scenarios. The techniques employed to carry it out should be consistent with this complexity and the level of assurance required by the board.

Risk is a function of likelihood and impact. The risk equation, to which we will return again and again, is:

Risk = Likelihood x Impact

This equation can be expanded to reflect the asset-threat-vulnerability method: that vulnerabilities are the exposure or weakness that a threat can exploit to compromise an asset and that, by 'likelihood', we simply mean the likelihood of the threat exploiting the vulnerability. Adopting the principle that the impact value is the full consequence of an asset being compromised (as will be discussed in chapter 11, we can restate the equation thus:

Risk = (probability of threat exploiting vulnerability) x (total impact cost of asset being exploited)

For either of these descriptions of risk, our risk assessment methodology needs to equip us to ascribe values to these factors. While there are many different approaches to this, they essentially break down into two: qualitative and quantitative.

Qualitative *versus* quantitative

In conducting the impact analysis, consideration should be given to the advantages and disadvantages of quantitative *versus* qualitative assessments. A quantitative methodology is one that uses (primarily) quantitative input, i.e. mathematical data, and a qualitative one uses primarily non-mathematical input.

The main advantage of the qualitative impact analysis is that it prioritises the risks and identifies areas for immediate improvement in addressing the vulnerabilities. The disadvantage of the qualitative analysis is that it does not provide specific quantifiable measurements of the magnitude of the impacts, thus making a cost-benefit analysis of any recommended controls difficult to calculate precisely.

The major advantage of a quantitative impact analysis is, therefore, that it provides a measurement of the magnitude of some (but not all) impacts that can be used in the cost-benefit analysis. We say 'but not all' because there are some impacts (loss of reputation, loss of credibility, loss of public confidence, etc.) that are extremely difficult, if not impossible, to quantify meaningfully. At best, one may only be able to apply qualitative measures, such as 'high' or 'very high', without even being able to quantify the meaning of the term.

A potential disadvantage of quantitative methodologies is that, depending on the numerical ranges used to describe the impacts, the meaning of the quantitative impact analysis may be unclear. BS 7799-3 makes it clear, however, that this sort of instance should be avoidable regardless of whether you are using qualitative or quantitative measures. It states: "It is essential that risk owners and assessors share a common understanding of the criteria and scales used to express consequence",[18] and later that the same is true of scales to express likelihood. We will return to this in the following sections.

ISO 27005 also explains that it is possible to combine the two approaches: "In practice, qualitative analysis is often used first to obtain a general indication of the level of risk and to reveal the major risks. Later, it can be necessary to

---

[18] BS 7799-3, Clause 6.4.2.

undertake more specific or quantitative analysis on the major risks because it is usually less complex and less expensive to perform quantitative rather than qualitative analysis."[19]

Quantitative risk analysis

This approach looks at two figures: one for the probability of an event occurring and the other the likely loss should it occur. A single figure is produced from these two elements, by simply multiplying the potential loss (measured in monetary terms) by its probability (measured as a percentage or fraction of times per year, say). This is sometimes called the annualised loss expectancy (ALE) or the estimated annual cost (EAC). Clearly, the higher the number that an event or risk has, the more serious it is for the organisation. It is then possible to rank risks in order of magnitude (ALE) and to make decisions based upon this.

The problem with this type of risk analysis is that so long can be taken producing a figure, and then revisiting the figures in light of comparison with other assets, threats and vulnerabilities, that no progress towards actual implementation of the ISMS is made. In some cases, this approach can promote or reflect complacency about the real significance of particular risks. The monetary value of the potential loss is also often subjectively assessed and, when the two components are multiplied together, the answer is equally subjective. A methodology that produces results that are largely dependent on subjective individual decisions, which are unlikely to be similar to the decisions of another person, is not one that will produce results that are

---

[19] ISO 27005, Clause 8.3.1.

reproducible and comparable and it will, therefore, fail the requirements of ISO 27001.

BS 7799-3 posits advice for reducing the impact of such subjectivity, notably in suggesting that likelihood and impact can be measured as exponential functions. That is, instead of trying to determine the precise value of an impact, accept that it will fall within a range that spans orders of magnitude. The organisation might, therefore, use the following scales:

Likelihood/frequency	Impact/consequence
Less than once per year	Up to £100
Every year	Up to £1,000
Every month	Up to £10,000
Every week	Up to £100,000
Every day	Up to £1,000,000
Every hour	More than £1,000,000

Under this scheme, you might determine that a risk will happen at least once a month and cost between £10,000 and £100,000. Scales such as these are unlikely to generate wildly different results across different assessors.

A number of organisations have successfully adopted quantitative risk analysis.

Qualitative risk analysis

BS 7799-3 provides guidance that the risk assessment methodology should enable the organisation to "estimate

2: Risk assessment methodologies

potential losses" and use this information to make decisions about proportionate security controls by taking into account "the relative costs and expected benefits of each control". This is supported by ISO 27000:2018, which states that "The expenditure on relevant controls is expected to be proportionate to the perceived business impact of the risk materializing."[20]

'Estimation' and 'proportionate' are two principles that form the basis of a qualitative risk assessment methodology, one that doesn't need a precisely calculated ALE. A qualitative methodology ranks identified risks in relation to one another, using a qualitative or hierarchical scale (such as: very serious – serious – bearable – not a problem). It is, therefore, based on similar qualitative hierarchies, or scales, of threat and vulnerability seriousness, and of likelihood and impact.

It is, of course, imperative that these terms are well understood by all risk assessors and risk owners. If risk assessments are to be repeatable and comparable, two risk assessors must be able to reach the same conclusions; and for risk treatments to be correctly (and proportionately) applied, the risk owners need to understand the severity of the risk.

One of the key concepts for risk assessment in the BS 7799-3 guidance is that consequences should be valued to take into account "the wider consequence that might result [from] breaches of legal, regulatory or statutory requirements" (Clause 6.4.2). It also says that "Events and consequences can often be determined by a discovery of the concerns of top management, risk owners and the requirements identified

---

[20] ISO/IEC 27000:2018, Clause 4.5.2.

in determining the context of the organisation" (Clause 7.2.2).

Significantly, BS 7799-3 states that "the design of a qualitative risk matrix should be driven by the risk acceptance criteria of the organization, rather than being assumed to conform to some arbitrary uniform layout" (Clause 6.4.4). It suggests that a standard valuation scale should be defined for impacts to assist risk assessors and risk owners. It does, however, state that "Although a qualitative risk matrix that is fully symmetrical about its low/low to high/high diagonal might naively seem desirable and is simple to create, it is unlikely to represent accurately any organization's real information security risk acceptance criteria."

ISO 27000 is less clear on this subject: it talks about risk identification as the "process of finding, recognizing and describing risks" (Clause 3.68); it defines a consequence as an "outcome of an event affecting objectives" (Clause 3.12). Impact and consequences are really different words for much the same concept, which is to establish the level of damage the organisation will suffer as a result of any given security breach.

ISO 27005, meanwhile, states that "Risk assessment is often conducted in two (or more) iterations. First, a high level assessment is carried out to identify potentially high risks that warrant further assessment. The next iteration can involve further in-depth consideration of potentially high risks revealed in the initial iteration. Where this provides insufficient information to assess the risk, then further detailed analyses are conducted" (Clause 8.1). This approach encourages the organisation to consider risk scales that change or adapt as the risk is better understood or to isolate the real scale of its consequences.

A qualitative methodology is by far the most widely used approach to risk analysis. As described for quantitative analysis, the risk level can be based on banding values or levels for likelihood and impact, so exact calculations are not required. ISO 27005 says that a qualitative methodology "uses a scale of qualifying attributes to describe the magnitude of potential consequences (e.g. low, medium and high)" (Clause 8.3.1). However, in order to ensure that the results are comparable and reproducible, the bands must be defined so that a medium impact in the judgement of one person is demonstrably comparable to a medium impact in another's. The output of the risk equation would then also be qualitative.

The output of a five-level risk scale, for instance, might lead to risks being placed on a scale that identifies them as:

Risk level	Risk treatment action required
Very high	Unacceptable: action needs to be taken immediately.
High	Unacceptable: action to be taken as soon as possible.
Medium	Action required and to be taken within a reasonable timescale.
Low	Acceptable: no action required as a result of risk assessment. Any action should be the subject of a full cost-benefit analysis.
Very low	Acceptable: no action required.

The output of the risk equation can be represented using a scale such as the three-level likelihood and impact version shown in Figure 3 (which produces a five-level risk scale), and which relates the identified impact of an event occurring to an assessed likelihood of it actually happening.

Likelihood	High	Medium risk	High risk	
	Medium	Low risk	Medium risk	High risk
	Low	Very low risk	Low risk	Medium risk
		Low	Medium	High

Impact

Figure 3: Three-level risk matrix

The methodology recommended by this book, and developed fully in chapter 7, is a qualitative one. Working methods for assessing impact, likelihood, threat and vulnerability are all important to the qualitative methodology, and the balance of this chapter will review the key concepts for each of these before we turn, in the next chapter, to their application in an ISO 27001 risk assessment.

One of the key, practical benefits of a qualitative risk assessment methodology is that it recognises that there is inevitably a subjective aspect to any risk assessment exercise, and it provides a framework in which such assessments can give comparable and reproducible results. It also allows you to complete the initial risk assessment within a reasonable time period, and accepts that, in assessing and controlling risk, it is preferable to be 'approximately correct, rather than precisely wrong'.

OCTAVE

One well-known approach that can be tailored to meet the requirements of ISO 27001 is the Operationally Critical Threat, Asset, and Vulnerability Evaluation (OCTAVE[21]) set of criteria, which provides useful input for any organisation developing its own practical approach. Note, however, that OCTAVE does not on its own meet the requirements of ISO 27001.

OCTAVE was developed by Carnegie Mellon University. It is a set of criteria that can be developed into many different methodologies, and can use either quantitative or qualitative approaches; as long as those methodologies adhere to the OCTAVE criteria, each is recognised as an OCTAVE-consistent method.

The OCTAVE criteria consist of a set of principles, attributes and outputs. These include the principle of self-direction (i.e. the risk assessment is resourced from within the organisation being assessed), using a multi-disciplinary team (an attribute), and that outputs will relate to three phases of assessment.

---

[21] See *https://resources.sei.cmu.edu/library/asset-view.cfm?assetID=309051.*

To apply OCTAVE, a small team from across the organisation works together to consider the security needs of the organisation while balancing operational risk, security practices and technology. This team is known as the analysis team.

OCTAVE factors all aspects of risk into decision-making. That is to say, it considers assets, threats, vulnerabilities and organisational impact and includes them in the process. OCTAVE requires the analysis team to follow a specific series of steps:

1. Identify information-related assets that are important to the organisation.

2. Focus risk analysis activities on those assets judged to be most critical.

3. Consider the relationships among critical assets, the threats to those assets, and vulnerabilities that can be exploited by the threats.

4. Evaluate risks in an operational context – considering how assets are used in the business and how those assets are at risk due to security threats.

5. Create a practical protection strategy for organisational improvement as well as risk mitigation plans to reduce the risk to the organisation's critical assets.

OCTAVE uses a three-phased approach to enable the analysis team to produce a comprehensive picture of the organisation's information security needs:

Phase 1: Build asset-based threat profiles – the analysis team determines which information-related assets are important to the organisation and identifies the arrangements (controls) that are currently in place to protect those assets.

They identify the assets that are most important to the organisation and describe the security requirements for each critical asset. They then identify threats to each of these assets, creating a threat profile for that asset. ISO 27001, in contrast, only describes a relatively abstract framework that focuses on identifying the risks and risk owners, and expects that all information security risks will be identified, thereby identifying all of the possible impacts.

Phase 2: Identify infrastructure vulnerabilities – the analysis team examines network access paths, identifying classes of information technology components related to each critical asset, and then determines the extent to which each class of component is resistant to network attacks.

Phase 3: Develop security strategy and plans – the analysis team identifies risks to the identified critical assets and decides what to do about them, creating mitigation plans to address the risks to the assets, based on the phase 1 and 2 analyses.

Carnegie Mellon University has developed three methodologies using the OCTAVE criteria: the original Octave method (which forms the basis of the Octave body of knowledge), for large and complex organisations or those split across a number of geographical locations; Octave-S for small organisations with between 20 and 80 people and which are not complex in structure; and Octave Allegro, a more streamlined approach for information security assessment and assurance.

Other methodologies

The Delphi Risk Assessment Method (DRAM) and the Facilitated Risk Assessment Process (FRAP) are also risk assessment methodologies. There are many others. ENISA lists some of the less widely used methodologies: *www.enisa.europa.eu/topics/threat-risk-management/risk-management/current-risk/risk-management-inventory*.

CHAPTER 3: RISK MANAGEMENT OBJECTIVES

We identified, in chapter 1, the probability that most organisations already have in place a range of risk assessment approaches, driven perhaps by regulation as much as by the board's desire to meet its fiduciary duties to shareholders and other stakeholders in the organisation.

Risk acceptance or tolerance

An organisation's risk acceptance criteria (which we discussed in chapter 1) are defined in its overall approach to risk management and are contained in its information security policy.

ISO 27001 says that the ISMS policy must be "compatible with the strategic direction of the organization" (Clause 5.1), which may include the organisation's ERM framework if it already has one in place. What this means is that the organisation, in order to focus effectively on managing risk, should not have a number of different levels of risk tolerance or risk acceptance. When an organisation approaches risk management on a piecemeal basis, with different individuals or departments leading different risk management efforts, without any common direction or guidance, it can easily find itself in a situation where it has, by default, a number of different levels of risk acceptance. These different levels are illustrated by the four curved lines in Figure 4.

Organisations that have different levels of risk tolerance for different aspects of their operations (e.g. information security, health and safety, financial control, operational risk) find it difficult to provide coherent management.

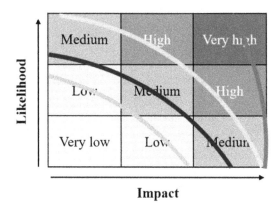

Figure 4: Inconsistent risk tolerance

Not all these different levels of risk acceptance, or of risk tolerance, are necessarily acceptable to the board. Organisations should, rather, set risk tolerance levels that are consistently applied through all their operations, irrespective of whether they are IT, financial or operational in nature. The ISO 27001 requirement that the risk assessment methodology should take the organisational context into account is designed exactly to ensure this level of coordination.

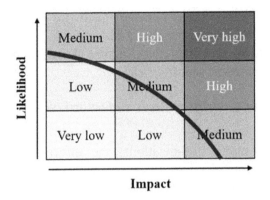

Figure 5: Risk tolerance or acceptance: criteria applied consistently across all activities

Information security risk management objectives

NIST's SP 800-30, *Guide for Conducting Risk Assessments*, is consistent with the ERM frameworks we have been discussing and is also reflected, as we shall see, in ISO 27001. It establishes four components of risk management: framing risk, assessing risk, responding to risk and monitoring risk. It states that the purpose of framing risk is to: "produce a risk management strategy that addresses how organizations intend to assess risk, respond to risk, and monitor risk—making explicit and transparent the risk perceptions that organizations routinely use in making both investment and operational decisions. The risk management strategy establishes a foundation for managing risk and delineates the boundaries for risk-based decisions within organizations."

In essence, one might say that an organisation's risk management objective is to ensure that there is a proper balance of safeguards against the risks of failing to meet business objectives: neither too much nor too little.[22] By extension, the risk management objective for an ISMS is to limit risk to an acceptable level across all information assets for all information security risks.

Information security controls and return on investment (ROI)

In all too many organisations, the information security controls historically adopted were selected on the basis of informed opinion, rather than as a result of a systematic and reproducible business-oriented risk assessment. There is, in fact, a direct relationship between the level of investment and the return on that investment: those organisations that under-invest in information security have as negative a return on their investment as do those organisations that over-invest in it.

Optimum ROI in information security control investment is driven by selecting and implementing those controls that will mitigate specific, identified risks to specific, identified assets, and whose total cost of implementation is lower than the potential cost of impact of the identified risk. Above all, those controls whose design is predicated on a proper understanding of the required balance between the confidentiality, integrity and availability (particularly to business users) of information are the most cost-effective and useful of controls.

---

[22] This is sometimes known as the 'Goldilocks solution'.

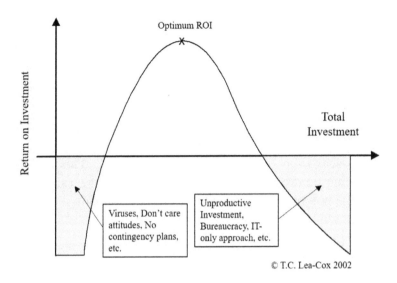

Figure 6: Return on investment in information security controls

The graph shown in Figure 6 demonstrates that too much investment in information security controls can be as bad as too little. However:

Simply removing existing information security controls or safeguards in order to improve the availability of information to business users may increase the risk of loss to unacceptable levels;

Having too many safeguards in place – a not infrequent characteristic of organisations where the board has abdicated its responsibility for information security control decisions to the IT department – quite often makes the information security system too expensive or bureaucratic, not just in respect of the direct cost of implementation but also in relation to the negative impact the safeguards have on business productivity; and

Risk assessment can be used as a method by which expenditure on security and contingency-planning can be justified.

The practical approach for organisations that want to maximise the return on their investment in information security controls is to select controls, having first analysed the likelihood of a compromise occurring, on the basis of their economic value to the organisation. This means selecting controls with specific reference to the value of – and the potential impact on the business of losing – specific information assets.

High-value assets – faced with high risks – should be protected by more extensive controls than low-value assets. While a scenario-based assessment might seem abstracted from this, the reality is that the impact of a given risk cannot be estimated without some appreciation of the assets that will be affected. As such, from at least an abstract level, the information security risk assessment operates at the asset level, and controls should only be selected and applied to those risks where management has determined that the potential loss to the organisation is such that investment in controls is appropriate.

This is an obviously sensible approach: it ensures that limited financial and human resources are prioritised and allocated to counter the biggest risks to the organisation, rather than applied indiscriminately across all assets of the organisation. An information security risk assessment quite often enables organisations to identify areas in which their controls are in excess of their real requirements and it, therefore, enables resources to be freed-up for reinvestment in more critical areas.

Typically, organisations attempt to simplify the risk assessment process by aggregating information assets and then identifying generic threats to that aggregation. This over-simplification, however, can lead to dissimilar assets being treated in the same manner, typically as if they all had the attributes of the most valuable, and/or most vulnerable, within the group and, as a result, the controls that are selected are not actually required for a number of items within the group. In such instances, it is obviously more valuable to treat risks at the individual asset level – individual laptops, servers, databases, folders, emails, records, and so on.

Risk management and process models

ISO 27001 is very clear about the risk management approach that it requires and where risk management sits in the project plan.

The previous iteration of ISO 27001 adopted the Plan-Do-Check-Act (PDCA) model, which anyone familiar with management systems and various change tools will recognise. The model is based on the idea that an organisation needs to 'plan' what it is going to do, carry out those plans (i.e. 'do' it), 'check' that what they have done has achieved the desired objective, and then 'act' on any shortfall.

Since 2013, ISO 27001 has not specified the process model that organisations must use, so they are now free to use PDCA or any other model they like. PDCA is well understood, however, so it remains popular.

PDCA applies to ISO 27001 implementation as follows:

Plan (establish the ISMS): establish the scope, security policy, targets, processes and procedures relevant to assessing risk and carry out risk assessment in order to improve information security so that it delivers results in accordance with the organisation's overall policies and objectives.

Do (implement and operate the ISMS): implement and operate the security policy, and the controls that were chosen as a result of the risk assessment process, as well as the processes and procedures of the ISMS.

Check (monitor and review the ISMS): assess and, where applicable, measure process performance against security policy, objectives and practical experience and report the results to management for review. This will include measuring the effectiveness of the management system and the controls that it implements.

Act (maintain and improve the ISMS): take corrective and preventive actions based on the results of the management review to achieve continual improvement of the ISMS.

Once the 'act' stage is completed the organisation then starts over again, planning what to do to improve the ISMS. Any other process model should also operate on a cyclical basis. It is, therefore, correct to say that an organisation that has embarked on an ISO 27001 project is in a continuum, and that the aim of this cyclic experience is to identify and manage risks, and drive continual improvement of the ISMS.

From the perspective of PDCA, risk assessment initially takes place during the planning stage of the ISO 27001 ISMS project. Control selection and implementation cannot start until after the risk assessment process is completed. Put another way, the risk assessment informs the management of risk and is thus critical to the creation of the risk treatment plan. The relationship between risk assessment and risk treatment, and their position on the PDCA continuum, is clear and is as shown in Figure 7.

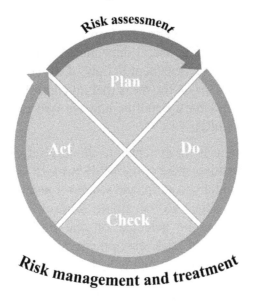

Figure 7: Risk management and the PDCA cycle

More accurately, we should say that risk assessment always falls totally within the 'plan' stage of the ISMS project cycle, and that some of the risk management, – in fact, the majority of the decision-making around control objectives and controls – is also within this stage, as that is what informs the risk treatment plan and the organisation's Statement of Applicability (SoA).[23] These, in turn, inform further the operational structure and content of the ISMS, which

---

[23] ISO 27001, Clause 6.1.3.

implements and manages the controls that bring the identified risks within an acceptable level.

The risk assessment, of course, also provides the organisation with a baseline for improvement. The extent to which this baseline is useful depends on whether you have conducted the risk assessment in light of the controls that are already in place, or on the basis that no controls are applied. Both approaches have benefits, and we will return to their pros and cons later.

Risk assessment is, in conclusion, the key activity required during the planning stage of the ISMS project – regardless of the process model you adopt and whatever name it assigns to the planning stage. Every single control that is to be implemented will be selected on the basis of the risk assessment, and the risk assessment must be completed before any controls are implemented. Risk assessment is also an ongoing activity of the ISMS; whenever there is a change in the risk environment, or of business requirements, or to the asset – indeed, whenever there is any change that might affect the risk profile of the asset – a new risk assessment will be required.

In fact, risk assessment is so central to information security management that we see it as the *core competence* of the ISMS.

PDCA and the risk acceptance criteria

While ISO 27001 expects the board to finalise its risk acceptance criteria and risk assessment methodology before the risk acceptance process itself is started, experience teaches that most organisations need to apply the PDCA (or other process model) principle to this aspect of their ISMS as well.

In other words, senior management and the board should determine, initially, what the acceptance criteria and methodology should be. It is not unusual for either excessive caution or unexpected bravado to underpin this initial phase of development work – not least because the total value or full nature of the organisation's information assets is not always fully appreciated at this early stage.

The initial methodology and risk acceptance criteria should then be applied in a test environment (the 'do' phase of the PDCA), with a reasonably wide range of information assets. These tests will lead to potential risk treatment decisions that management and the board can assess (the 'check' phase) for reasonableness and acceptability in light of the broader risk management and investment context. The methodology and criteria can then be revised to produce results that are more acceptable to management and this then becomes the 'release' version.

It is worth retaining this perspective throughout the risk assessment process so that, if results are generated that seem out of line with common sense, the risk assessor can revert to the risk assessment criteria and methodology and, if necessary, propose improvements to it. Of course, improvements – and the reasons for them – should be documented and will form part of the ISMS documentation.

CHAPTER 4: ROLES AND RESPONSIBILITIES

Risk management is a process that involves people. While many of the people involved in this process will already have specific responsibilities inside the organisation, it is important to identify precisely the contribution they are expected to make to the risk management process.

ISO 27001 requires (Clause 5.3) that "Top management shall ensure that the responsibilities and authorities for roles relevant to information security are assigned and communicated." This sentiment is supported by ISO 27005 (Clause 7.4), which states that "The organization and responsibilities for the information security risk management process should be set up and maintained." This must, obviously, include apportioning key duties in relation to risk management.

Senior management commitment

Without senior-level management commitment it is unlikely an ISO 27001 project would get as far as a risk assessment, but if it did, it certainly would not get much further.

In our experience, the risk assessment stage of the project is one of the most testing. The sheer amount of time and effort required to undertake a risk assessment that is sufficiently detailed to meet the requirements of ISO 27001 is always underestimated at the start of the project, and this is when the drive and clout of senior management commitment are essential. That is, of course, assuming the senior managers understood what they were committing to in the first place!

4: Roles and responsibilities

One of the first things the project team should stage, in any ISMS project, is a board briefing that ensures the senior managers who are signing up to the project, and committing the resources and effort to achieve the objective of certification (or at least an ISO 27001-conforming ISMS), do so from an adequately informed position.

Of course, this means that they need to be aware of the costs and amount of work required, but also the benefits that follow, including the indirect benefits of, for example, identifying and protecting specific information assets, and of changing and improving the mindset of those managers responsible for them. In some organisations, just producing an information asset register is a major undertaking and can warrant a considerable project in its own right, delivering benefits when the invoices and 'Friday cake club' schedule are suitably segregated and asset 'owners' identified.

As this book explains, the risk assessment process will involve a number of staff for a considerable amount of time. When done correctly, management and senior staff will be involved and their time will suddenly become all the more precious. When senior management makes an adequately informed commitment to the project, sufficient encouragement and resources should be made available for the project to progress to plan and to time.

Another benefit and product of senior management commitment should be the assignment of a dedicated resource for coordinating risk management policies and tasks. Assigning a central risk management coordination resource (which we discuss further, below) is a critical success factor. The intention is that this central focal point carries out coordination activities, acts as a route for risk issues to be brought to the attention of senior management, ensures suitable tools and resources are available, and provides guidance and advice to all those elsewhere in the business who are actually carrying out the risk assessment activities.

Not only does such a central resource ensure that risk management receives the attention it deserves both initially and subsequently but it also provides the essential structure by which risk assessment results throughout the organisation can be confirmed as "consistent, valid and comparable" – a key requirement of the risk assessment methodology as defined in ISO 27001.

The (lead) risk assessor

It is entirely up to the individual organisation to choose who is to undertake, or rather coordinate, the risk assessment, and how. There are two issues to consider before deciding who. The first is that the Standard expects that periodic reviews of security risks and related controls will be carried out – taking account of new threats and vulnerabilities, assessing the impact of changes in the business, its goals or processes, technology and/or its external environment (such as legislation, regulation or society), and simply to confirm that controls remain effective and appropriate. Periodic review is a fundamental requirement of any risk assessment or risk management strategy.

The second issue is that the Standard requires the organisation to "determine the necessary competence of person(s) doing work under its control that affect its information security performance" and "ensure that these persons are competent on the basis of appropriate education, training, or experience". It is, therefore, essential that the risk assessment is managed by an appropriately qualified and experienced person. This is logical: the key step on which the entire ISMS will be built needs, itself, to be solid. The ISO 27001 auditor will want to see documentary evidence of the formal qualifications and experience of this person; at least that they have been reviewed and accepted by management.

A number of organisations will, as we have seen, already have a risk management function, staffed by people with training that enables them to carry out risk assessments. The role of the risk management team is, usually, to systematically identify, evaluate and control potential losses to the organisation that may result from things that haven't happened yet. The skills and methodology available to this group may or may not also meet the requirements of ISO 27001. Either way, there are potentially significant benefits for such an organisation if its information security risk assessments can be carried out by the same function that handles all risk assessments.

The benefits lie not just in cost effectiveness, but in the fact that such a risk management, or risk control resource, will have an existing and ongoing understanding of the business, its goals and environment, and an appreciation of all the risks faced by the business in the pursuit of its objectives. Equally, they should be able to assess how all the different risks, and the steps taken to counter them, are related and coordinated. This, of course, also helps address the requirement that the risk assessment is conducted in the context of the wider business.

Many organisations, however, do not have an internal risk management function. There are two possible ways to tackle the issue of risk assessment. The first is to hire an external consultant (or firm of consultants) to do it. The second is to train someone internally to do it. The second is preferable in most cases, as the risk assessment "shall perform information security risk assessments at planned intervals or when significant changes are proposed or occur" and having the expertise in-house enables this to be undertaken cost-effectively. It also increases ownership of the process and the resulting ISMS.

In circumstances where the organisation has existing arrangements with external suppliers for risk assessment services, or is in the process of setting up a risk management function or capability (in the context of responding to the requirements of the increasing corporate governance and regulatory requirements, perhaps), then it should, from the outset, investigate ways in which its risk assessment processes could be integrated.

It is more difficult for a smaller business to retain specialist information security expertise in-house than for a larger one; the internal risk assessment role needs to be maintained over time and the person concerned needs to continue being trained and involved in both information security and risk assessment issues, both inside and outside the organisation.

The disadvantage of hiring external risk assessors, apart from the cost, is that the organisation does not necessarily get continuity of involvement from individuals within a firm of assessors. The advantage of the external hire, apart from it being a variable cost, is that the external assessor should be up to date on relevant issues and should be wholly objective. A possible middle route is to contract on a multi-year basis, with an appropriately trained individual or consultancy firm to personally provide this service as and when it is required, working closely with identified internal staff. However the organisation chooses to acquire this resource, it is crucial that they are in place and able to be fully involved in the risk analysis and assessment process that this book describes.

Other roles and responsibilities

We have already said, categorically, that board and senior management support for the ISMS and, by extension, for the risk management process is critical. However, senior management support on its own will not be sufficient for the organisation to succeed: responsibilities need to be devolved to a number of people throughout the organisation. The risk assessment process will rely on input from a wide range of sources, and all those people who are most able to provide knowledgeable and informed input and decisions must contribute to the process.

The people who should support[24] and participate in the risk management process include:

Chief information officer (CIO): is responsible for providing advice and other assistance to senior management to ensure that technology is acquired and that information resources are used in keeping with relevant laws, regulations and organisational priorities. Decisions made in these areas should be based on an effective risk management programme. Unless the CIO has substantial business experience and can communicate effectively and convincingly across the business-technology gulf that exists in most organisations, the CIO should not lead the ISO 27001 project. Achieving ISO 27001 is a business change project, not an IT project.

---

[24] NIST SP 800-30 provided the basis for several of the detailed role descriptions used here.

Senior executive management: are accountable to the board and have ultimate operational responsibility for achieving the organisation's goals. They must be committed to the project and must, therefore, ensure that the necessary resources are effectively applied to develop the capabilities needed to accomplish those goals. They must also assess and incorporate the results of the initial and ongoing risk assessment activity into their decision-making process. An effective risk management programme that assesses and mitigates information-related risks requires the support and involvement of senior management – without whose active and committed involvement an ISO 27001 project is, in any case, doomed to fail.

Risk owners: are granted the authority to manage a risk, and are therefore accountable for ensuring that it is done. This is a specific role set out in ISO 27001, and includes being responsible for approving the risk treatment plan and whatever residual risk will remain after treatment. As such, a great deal of communication and consultation around the management of risks will necessarily involve the risk owners, so they will need to be carefully chosen taking into account their proximity to the risk and their aptitude for cooperating with other roles involved in risk management.

Business managers (who are also likely to be information asset 'owners'): are responsible for determining the criticality and sensitivity of business operations and, therefore, of the information assets on which those business operations depend. Business managers are best placed to assess the real asset value that will inform the impact side of the risk assessment equation.

Business and functional managers: those responsible for business operations and the procurement process; they must also take an active role in the risk management process. These managers are the individuals with the authority and responsibility for making the trade-off decisions essential to achieving business objectives. Their involvement in the risk management process helps deliver effective security for the information systems, helping the organisation achieve its objectives with minimal expenditure on resources.

Information security officers (ISOs), information security managers and computer security officers: are responsible for their organisation's information security activity, including the implementation of risk treatment decisions. ISOs should all be appropriately qualified; appropriate qualifications are those (such as CISM®, CISMP) that are focused on managing information security, rather than its technical implementation.[25] ISOs have a leading role to play in introducing an appropriate, structured methodology that helps identify, evaluate and minimise risks to the information assets and IT systems that support the organisational objectives. Critically, therefore, ISOs must have risk assessment competence and the organisation needs to have made adequate provision for risk assessment training.

ISOs can also act internally as key consultants in support of senior management to help ensure the success of the ISMS project.

---

[25] See *www.itgovernance.co.uk/infosec/infosec_quals* for all the key information security management qualifications and graduate/postgraduate courses. Each qualification has different strengths and weaknesses; it is not unusual for individuals to accumulate more than one qualification.

IT security practitioners (including network, system, application and database administrators, computer specialists, security analysts and security consultants): are responsible for the proper implementation of control requirements in their IT systems. IT security practitioners should be appropriately skilled and trained, and should have relevant, current technical qualifications (e.g. CCNA, CCSA) related to those technologies for which they are specifically responsible.

As changes occur in the existing IT system environment (e.g. expansion in network connectivity, changes to the existing infrastructure and organisational policies, or the introduction of new technologies), the IT security practitioners must support or use the risk management process to identify and assess new potential risks and implement new security controls as needed to safeguard their IT systems.

Technical/functional personnel: are most able to form practical and realistic opinions on the likelihood of occurrence of the threat-vulnerability combinations that will be identified. Technical personnel include all those with relevant technical or functional expertise, including the facilities management team for physical security issues, HR for personnel, IT for information technology, those with responsibilities for utilities and other aspects of the corporate infrastructure, the finance team, the audit team, etc.

System and information asset owners: may be risk owners, but there is no specific requirement for this to be the case. Under previous versions of ISO 27001, asset owners played a key role in risk management, but they have now been largely supplanted by the risk owner. Despite this, asset owners are, practically speaking, likely to play an important role in managing controls to protect the confidentiality, integrity and availability of the information systems and information assets (data) they own. Typically, the system and information owners are also responsible for changes to their information assets. Thus, they might have to approve and sign off changes to their information systems (e.g. system enhancements, major changes to the software and hardware). The system and information owners must, therefore, understand their role in the risk management process and fully support it. Because of their familiarity with the assets they own, they will often play a critical role in risk assessments, providing the risk assessor(s) with information about threats, vulnerabilities, and the likelihood and impact of risks.

Training team: this should include subject matter experts and the champion users of the organisation's information systems, and these people have a key role to play. Use of the information systems and data according to an organisation's policies, guidelines and specific procedures are critical to mitigating risk and protecting the organisation's resources. To minimise risk to the information systems, it is essential that system and application users be provided with security awareness training. Therefore, the information security trainers or security/subject matter professionals must understand the risk management process, so that they can develop appropriate training materials and incorporate risk assessment into training programmes that are effective for the end users. Much of this training can be delivered through online learning or other media that ensures consistent delivery of a clearly articulated training message.

CHAPTER 5: RISK ASSESSMENT SOFTWARE

There are software tools that have been designed to assist in risk assessment and, although the Standard does not mandate their use, it is practically impossible to carry out and maintain a useful risk assessment for an organisation that has more than about four workstations without using such a tool. It is essential that the risk assessment be completed methodically, systematically and comprehensively. An appropriate software tool designed with ISO 27001 in mind and kept up to date in terms of changing information security issues can be effective in this process.

The risk assessment is a complex and data-rich process and is made enormously simpler if you can use ready-made databases of threats and vulnerabilities. Whether you take an asset-based or scenario-based approach to risk assessment, these can be assigned as necessary and given relevant impact and likelihood values to significantly speed up the process.

The database should also contain details of the control decisions made as a result of the risk assessment, so that, at a glance, it is easy to see what controls are in place for each asset or scenario within the ISMS.

This database must be updated in the light of new risk assessments, which should take place whenever there are changes to the assets or to any aspect of the risk environment. The number of software tools available for this purpose is increasing. To one extent or another, they streamline the risk assessment process and generate the SoA. In theory, such a tool ought to encourage the user to perform a thorough and comprehensive security audit on the organisation's information systems, and ought not to produce too much paperwork as a result. Tool availability is likely to change as the Standard is more widely taken up and any organisation interested in pursuing this route should, therefore, do up-to-date research on what is available before making a shortlist.

The organisation may need to compare tools before making a selection and should concentrate, in the comparison process, on the extent to which the tool really does easily and effectively streamline the risk assessment and SoA development process, the amount of additional paperwork it generates, the flexibility it offers for dealing with changing circumstances and frequent, smaller-scale risk assessments, and the meaningfulness of the results it generates.

Tracking changes to the risk assessment process over time is also important, and often the 'future-proofing' aspect of requirements of the tool are overlooked during the initial purchase because of the focus on achieving certification, or at least the implementation of an ISO 27001-compliant ISMS. Of course, normal due diligence analyses should also be undertaken of the status of the supplier and manufacturer of the product to ensure that it is properly supported and likely to continue to be.

Risk assessments can be done without using such tools, although it can be difficult to demonstrate that the risk assessment produces comparable and reproducible results without one. A proper risk assessment in any business will be very time consuming, whether or not a software tool is used. 'Time consuming' means one or more months of dedicated work, and even longer for larger organisations. The use of a software tool will depend on the organisation's culture and the preferences of the information security adviser and manager.

Practically speaking, once the organisation has decided to purchase such a tool, it becomes dependent on that tool and on the staff members who are trained to use it. In considering the appropriate route forward, take into account the likelihood of being able to recruit staff who have broad risk assessment experience and can adapt to the organisation's environment as against the likelihood of recruiting and retaining staff who have specific experience with one risk assessment tool, if that tool requires particular specialist knowledge.

If the organisation decides to purchase such a tool, the ISMS project steering group should document the reasons for its choice and selection. Whoever is to use it will, of course, have to be fully competent in its use. Evidence of any training and of the level of proficiency achieved should be retained on the personnel file of the person trained in its use.

It is essential to appreciate that risk assessment tools are a specific type of tool, different from other tools, such as gap analysis tools, vulnerability assessment tools or penetration testing.

Gap analysis tools

It is important to understand the difference between a gap analysis and an ISO 27001-compliant risk assessment. A risk assessment seeks to identify risks to the organisation, to analyse them and to evaluate them for treatment in accordance with the organisation's needs; a gap analysis assesses the gap between the requirements of a standard or other set of requirements (such as a risk treatment plan or SoA) and the measures that are actually in place. Such gap analysis tools almost invariably analyse the gap between the processes and measures in place in an organisation and the complete set of those required by the standard. While this exercise can be interesting, and potentially valuable for assessing the effort that could be involved in an implementation project, it is not a practical replacement for a risk assessment.

A gap analysis will fall short of a risk assessment where ISO 27001 is concerned because not all organisations are likely to need to implement all the controls identified in the Standard. An analysis of the gap between the controls listed in Annex A of ISO 27001 and the current implementation status is not, therefore, particularly useful in the creation of an ISO 27001-compliant ISMS.

There is no point in attempting to use such a tool to carry out the risk assessment component of the ISMS project, because it simply doesn't meet the requirements of the Standard.

Vulnerability assessment tools

Vulnerability assessment tools,[26] also called security scanning tools, are also not risk assessment tools as defined by the Standard. They may well be used as part of the risk assessment process in order to identify vulnerabilities, and they do have a role to play in many ISMSs – a role determined by the risk treatment plan that arises from the risk assessment.

Vulnerability assessment tools assess the security of network or host systems and report system vulnerabilities. These tools are designed to scan networks, servers, firewalls, routers and software applications for vulnerabilities. Generally, the tools can detect known security flaws or bugs in software and

---

[26] See the discussion of technical vulnerability controls in chapter 9.

hardware, determine if the systems are susceptible to known attacks and exploits, and search for system vulnerabilities, such as settings contrary to established security policies.

In evaluating a vulnerability assessment tool, consider how frequently it is updated to include the detection of new weaknesses, security flaws and bugs, and whether or not it refers to common lists of flaws and vulnerabilities, such as the SANS Top Cyber Security Risks, CVE and Bugtraq. Vulnerability assessment tools are not usually run in real time, but are commonly run on a periodic basis. The tools can generate both technical and management reports, including text, charts and graphs. Vulnerability assessment reports can identify what weaknesses exist and how to fix them.

For many organisations, it is generally more practical to contract vulnerability scanning out to a third party than to necessarily maintain the tool and the expertise internally.

Penetration testing

Penetration testing (or pen testing) is also not a risk assessment. A penetration test is a snapshot of the organisation's security at a specific point in time. It can test the effectiveness of security controls and preparedness measures. While a vulnerability assessment is usually an automated process, penetration testing usually involves a team of (external) experts who test and identify an information system's vulnerability to attack. They may attempt to bypass security controls by exploiting identified vulnerabilities using, for instance, social engineering, denial-of-service (DoS) attacks and other methods. The objective of a penetration test is to locate system vulnerabilities so that appropriate corrective steps can be taken.

Pen testing does, therefore, have a role to play in the ISO 27001 risk assessment; it has an even more substantial role to play after the assessment, to test the effectiveness of defences that have been installed and to ensure that technical controls are performing as they are expected to.

Risk assessment tools

Not all of those tools that currently claim to be ISO 27001 risk assessment tools are necessarily so, and those that are may not meet your requirements. Different tools target different organisational profiles and are sold under various licence arrangements. Aspects to consider in determining the most suitable tool for any one project should include:

- The platform the tool is to run on (laptop, server, ASP server, the Cloud, etc.);

- The scope of compliance of the standard (ISO/IEC 27001:2013, ISO/IEC 27002:2013, NIST SP 800-30, the PCI DSS, etc.);

- Scalability (to the needs of the organisation and to the number of users);

- Flexibility (the ability to divide the process into various sections and run them as discrete assessments in their own right, e.g. for business units, or for specific IT systems, or after change to an asset, and then the option to analyse the wider impact on full assessment);

- Import (of, for instance, asset lists) and export facility;

- Customisable reporting, to suit organisational structures;

- Degree of alignment with ISO 27001 or with establishing an ISMS (especially any support in producing an SoA);

- Licence model;

- Ease of use (because the more training that is required, the higher the total cost of ownership, particularly when you consider backup expertise);

- Price; and

- Any requirements for integrating the risk assessment results with another risk management regime.

We have identified the following software tools, each of which claims (to one extent or another) to be an information security risk assessment tool:

CyberWatch

www.riskwatch.com

vsRisk Cloud

www.vigilantsoftware.co.uk

Risk assessment tool descriptions[27]

RiskWatch meets many of the requirements identified earlier in this chapter. It has an effective, comprehensive risk assessment methodology and can assess risk both quantitatively and qualitatively. While it was not built

---

[27] The information contained in this section is derived from our own research. Within the limitations of research carried out in a competitive marketplace, it was valid at the time of the assessment. We emphasise that these are our own assessments; any reader who wishes to review the tools is encouraged to do so.

specifically for ISO 27001 work, or the establishment and management of an ISMS, it claims that it can apply both ISO 27002 and NIST SP 800-53[28] controls, and can be either PC- or server-based. While it appears to be a first-class tool, it also, tellingly, does not list its price. Several years ago, however, a single-user licence cost US$14,500. It is probably best suited to larger organisations that require a more sophisticated and granular approach to risk quantification, and to organisations with a US exposure (or that are based in North America), because NIST SP 800-53 compliance is not a common requirement outside the US. It is also useful to risk consultants whose offering includes sophisticated, detailed risk assessments at this level.

vsRisk Cloud has been designed specifically for ISO 27001 risk assessments, and includes a number of control sets, notably ISO 27001:2005, ISO 27001:2013 and the PCI DSS. Uniquely, it is also in line with the guidelines of BS 7799-3, and both NIST SP 800-30 and SP 800-53. It was originally developed by a specialist risk management software company[29] to a project brief prepared by the authors of this book. It is now available as a Cloud-based application, which solves many of the problems that arise when using software over a network, as well as ensuring that it is available for reference in case of disaster or threats to business continuity. The features of vsRisk Cloud include the following:

- A wizard-based approach to simplify and accelerate the process for undertaking risk assessments.

---

[28] NIST SP 800-53, *Security and Privacy Controls for Information Systems and Organizations*.
[29] Vigilant Software Ltd – *www.vigilantsoftware.co.uk*.

- The ability to conduct asset-by-asset or scenario-based assessments, including granular identification of threats and vulnerabilities.

- A process to assign all relevant ISO 27001 Annex A controls.

- Integrated ISO 27005- and BS 7799-3-compliant threat and vulnerability databases, which are continually updated to ensure that they are the most up-to-date available anywhere.

- Customisable management scale and risk acceptance criteria.

- The ability to help define the scope and business requirements, policy and objectives for the ISMS.

- The ability to produce an audit-ready SoA.

- A detailed gap analysis that helps drive forward the risk treatment plan.

- Integrated audit trail and comparative history.

- The ability to help develop an ISMS asset inventory.

- The ability to capture business, legal and contractual requirements against each asset.

- The ability to assess confidentiality, integrity and availability against each asset.

- A built-in intuitive help feature.

- Asset monitor supports import and export of asset information.

- Backup and restore capability.

vsRisk Cloud has been designed to support an ISO 27001-compliant risk assessment beyond the first implementation cycle and has a clear user interface. It helps to ensure that the ISO 27001 risk assessment job is done correctly, easily and efficiently, time after time.

Conclusions

Our view is that, for most organisations, and for consultants providing ISMS services to most organisations, the most appropriate tool – in terms of functionality, ease of use and value for money – is the one that is completely in line with the requirements of ISO 27001, as well as all other national and international standards on information security risk assessment: vsRisk Cloud.

CHAPTER 6: INFORMATION SECURITY POLICY AND SCOPING[30]

While risk assessment is the core competence of information security, it is the information security policy and the agreed scope of the ISMS that provide the organisational context within which that risk assessment takes place. The first step in the planning phase for the establishment of an ISMS is the definition of the information security policy. A risk assessment can only be carried out once an information security policy exists to provide context and direction for the risk assessment activity.

Information security policy

This requirement is set out in Clause 5.2 of ISO 27001[31] (and control A.5.1 in Annex A of ISO 27001). It is not always, however, as straightforward as it seems. It may be an

---

[30] Much of this chapter reiterates (but does not replace) content that is already in *IT Governance: An International Guide to Data Security and ISO27001/ISO27002* (Kogan Page, 2019), and is repeated here to provide context for the further contents of this book. Readers are encouraged to read the original book for the full value of the contents of this chapter.

[31] Readers who do not already have copies of both ISO/IEC 27001:2013 and ISO/IEC 27002:2013 should obtain their own copies and read them. The standards are the key documents against which accredited certification is carried out. Copies of the standards (in either paper or downloadable format) can be obtained from national standards bodies and from the IT Governance online shop (*www.itgovernance.co.uk/standards*).

iterative process (particularly in complex organisations dealing with complex information security issues and/or multiple domains) and the final form of security policy that is adopted may, therefore, have to reflect the final risk assessment that has been carried out and the SoA that emerges from that.

Clause 5.2 sets out clearly the parameters of the ISMS policy. The policy must take into account the characteristics of the business, its organisation, location, assets and technology. The policy must either set or include a framework for setting its information security objectives, and establish the overall sense of direction. It must take into account all relevant business, legal, regulatory and contractual information security requirements. It must establish the strategic context (for the organisation and for its approach to risk management) within which the ISMS will be established. It must make commitments to the organisation's information security, its obligations and its continual improvement. It must be formally approved by senior management.

A statement that the board and management 'are committed to preserving the confidentiality, integrity and availability of information' will be at the heart of a security policy and an ISMS. It is important to define precisely the key terms used in the policy, and we recommend using the definitions contained in ISO 27000. ISO 27000 defines information very widely:

> Information is an asset that, like other important business assets, is essential to an organization's business and, consequently, needs to be suitably protected. Information can be stored in many forms, including: digital form (e.g. data files stored on electronic or optical media), material

form (e.g. on paper), as well as unrepresented information in the form of knowledge of the employees.[32]

In other words, appropriate protection is required for *all* forms of information and related assets.

Confidentiality [is defined as the] property that information is not made available or disclosed to unauthorized individuals, entities or processes.[33]

Integrity [is defined as the] property of accuracy and completeness.[34]

Availability [is defined as the] property of being accessible and usable upon demand by an authorized entity.[35]

Availability is particularly important to businesses engaged in e-commerce. A business whose very existence depends on the availability of its website, but which fails to take adequate steps to ensure that the site is up, running and running properly at all times, is likely to fail as a business much more quickly than a traditional bricks and mortar business that is unable to open its shop doors for a few days.

The board, management team and staff of the organisation should all understand that these are the definitions of these words and they should be prominently set out in the early briefings to staff and in internal communications. Auditors from certification bodies are likely to check (probably randomly) that staff understand what these words mean and,

---

[32] ISO 27000:2018, Clause 4.2.2.
[33] ISO 27000:2018, Clause 3.10.
[34] ISO 27000:2018, Clause 3.36.
[35] ISO 27000:2018, Clause 3.7.

while they will not look for staff to remember verbatim these definitions, will want staff to demonstrate a practical understanding of how the pursuit of these aspects of information security is likely to impact their own work. This level of understanding is required, as a minimum, so that each member of staff is able to recognise and react appropriately to a security incident.

The organisation will also need to define which physical and digital assets are to be covered by the policy. The kinds of technology employed and the basis on which the organisation operates will also strongly influence the scope of the ISMS.

The information security policy will also have to be regularly reviewed and updated in the light of changing circumstances, environment and experience. As a minimum, if there is no earlier reason for the board to review its policy, it should be reviewed annually and the board should agree that the policy remains appropriate (or otherwise) to its needs in the light of any changes to the business context, the risk assessment criteria or in the identified risks. There may be components of the policy that ought to be reviewed very regularly – even monthly – and these should be identified through the risk assessment.

Initially, the information security policy is a short statement (we think organisations should aim for a maximum of two pages of A4) that is designed to set out clearly the strategic aims and control objectives that will guide the development of the ISMS. The policy may go through a number of stages of development, particularly in the light of the risk assessment, but the final version must satisfy Clause 5.2 – and Annex A control 5.1.1 – of ISO 27001, as well as appropriately reflecting the good practice set out in Clause 5 of ISO 27002. The guidance in the introduction to ISO 27002 should also have been read and taken into account.[36] Proof that the policy has been approved by management, published and communicated internally, and that it is reviewed regularly (usually annually, as a minimum), with any changes similarly published and communicated, will enable the organisation to fully satisfy control objective A.5.1 of the Standard (Management direction for information security).

A copy of that section of the minutes (preferably initialled by the chairman as a correct copy) of the board meeting, in which the information security policy was debated and adopted, should be filed with the security policy documentation. It can be a controlled document and it does, for audit purposes, provide useful and immediate evidence of the process by which the policy was adopted, and of any amendments to it. This, together with the proposal that was put to the board, is the first part of the evidence that Clause 7.5.1 (Documented information – General) of the Standard requires in order to demonstrate that the requirements of the Standard have been implemented.

The policy itself should then be issued as a controlled document and made available to all who fall within its scope; as a minimum, members of the senior management team should receive individual copies and copies should be posted on all internal noticeboards, both the physical and electronic ones. These copies of the policy document should, of course,

---

[36] The information security policy template in the ISO 27001 ISMS Documentation Toolkit is drafted specifically to meet all these requirements and, like other top-level documents within the toolkit, needs minimal adaptation to meet the needs of individual organisations (see *www.itgovernance.co.uk/shop/product/iso-27001-iso27001-isms-documentation-toolkit*).

be clearly marked as controlled copies, to ensure that they are updated to reflect any changes that take place. Copies handed out, as part of training or awareness seminars, should be marked as uncontrolled copies.

Scope of the ISMS

Those parts of the organisation, and possibly beyond, to which the policy is going to apply need to be clearly identified. This may be done in part on the basis of corporate, divisional or management structure, or on the basis of geographic location. The other aspect of scope that needs to be considered is the logical boundary. A virtual organisation or a dispersed, multi-site operation may have different security issues from one located on a single site. In practical terms, a security policy that encompasses all of the activities within a specific entity, for which a specific board of directors or management team is responsible, is more easily implemented than one that is to be applied to only part of the entity. It is important to ensure that the board of directors that is implementing the policy does actually have adequate control over the operations specified within the policy and that it will be able to give a clear mandate to its management team to implement it.

It is essential to decide the boundary within which the ISMS is to provide assurance. The business environment and the Internet are each so huge and diverse that it is necessary to draw a boundary between what is within the organisation and what is without. In simple terms, boundaries are physically or logically identifiable. Boundaries have to be identified in terms of the organisation, or part of the organisation, that is to be protected, which networks and which data, and at which geographic locations.

The key components of defining the scope of the ISMS are:

- Identifying the boundaries or perimeters (physical and logical) of what is to be protected;

- Identifying all the systems necessary for the reception, storage, manipulation and transmission of information or data within those boundaries and the information assets within those systems;

- Identifying the relationships between these systems, the information assets and the organisational objectives and tasks; and

- Identifying the systems and information assets that are critical to the achievement of these organisational objectives and tasks and, if possible, ranking them in order of priority.

Clause A.8.1 is the ISO 27001:2013 Annex A control category that deals with the asset inventory, and the guidance of Clause 8.1 of ISO 27002:2013 should be followed at this point. It identifies clearly the classes or types of information asset that should be considered, and recommends that the information security classification of the asset be determined at this time – which would be sensible, given control category A.8.2's focus on appropriately classifying information.

The first step, therefore, is to identify which organisational entity is within the scope of the ISMS. The entity that is within the scope must be capable of physical and/or logical separation from third parties and from other organisations within a larger group. While this does not exclude third-party contractors, it does make it practically very difficult (although not necessarily impossible) to put an ISMS in place within an organisation that shares significant network and/or information assets or geographic locations. A division of a larger organisation that, for instance, shares a group head office and head office functions with other divisions, could not practically implement a meaningful ISMS.

Usually, the smallest organisational entity that is capable of implementing an ISMS is one that is self-contained. It will have its own board of directors or management team, its own functional support, its own premises and its own IT network.

The information that should be collected in order to clarify what will – and what won't – be within the scope of the ISMS will relate to:

- Hardware;
- Software;
- System interfaces (e.g. internal and external connectivity);
- Data and information;
- Persons who support and use the IT systems;
- System mission (i.e. the processes performed by the systems);
- System and data criticality (e.g. the system's value or importance to the organisation);
- System and data sensitivity;
- Functional requirements of the IT system;
- Users of the system (e.g. system users who provide technical support to the IT system, application users who use the IT system to perform business functions);
- System security policies governing the IT system;

- System security architecture;
- Current network topology (e.g. network diagram);
- Information storage protection;
- Flow of information pertaining to the IT system (e.g. system interfaces, system input and output flow charts);
- Technical controls used in the IT system;
- Management controls used in the IT system;
- Operational controls used in the IT system;
- Physical security environment of the IT system; and
- Environmental security implemented for the IT system.

Information gathered about some or all of these issues will help clarify what should be in the scope of the ISMS.

It is possible for divisions of larger organisations to independently pursue certification. The critical factor is the extent to which they can be practically differentiated from other divisions of the same parent organisation, and can exercise practical control over their information assets and over the implementation of controls that their risk assessment determines are necessary to protect those assets.

For larger organisations with a multiplicity of systems and extensive geographic spread, it is, as a general rule, often simpler to tackle ISO 27001 and, in particular, risk assessment, on the basis of smaller business units that meet the general description set out above. On the other hand, larger organisations that have a single business culture and largely common systems throughout are probably better off creating a single ISMS.

Once the organisational scope is identified, it is necessary to list the physical premises that the chosen organisation occupies and to identify its network and information assets.

If there are aspects of the organisation's activities or systems that are to be excluded from the requirements of the security policy, it is critical that these are clearly identified – and explained – at this stage. Multi-site or virtual organisations will need to carefully consider the different security requirements of their different sites and their management implications. There should be clear boundaries (defined in terms of the characteristics of the organisation, its location, assets and technology) within which the security policy and ISMS will apply.

Any exclusions should be openly debated by the board and the steering group, and the minutes should set out how and why the decision – for or against – was taken. It is possible that, in fact, divisions of the organisation, components of the information system or specific assets will not be able to be excluded from the scope, either because they are already so integral to it, or because their exclusion might undermine the information security objectives themselves. It must, therefore, be clear that any exclusions do not, in any way, undermine the security of the organisation to be assessed.

Certification auditors will be assessing how management applies its information security policy across the whole of the organisation that is defined as being within the scope of the policy. They should be expected to test to their limits the boundaries of the stated scope to ensure that all interdependencies and points of weakness have been identified and adequately dealt with.

In reality, as stated earlier, the process of designing and implementing an effective ISMS may be made simpler by including, within the scope, the entire organisation for which the board has responsibility.

There is an argument, in large, complex organisations, for a phased approach to implementation. Where it really is possible to adequately define a subsidiary part of the organisation, such that its information security needs can be independently assessed, it may be possible to gain substantial experience in designing and implementing an ISMS, as well as a track record of success and the momentum that accompanies it, so that a subsequent rollout to the rest of the organisation can be carried through successfully and smoothly. These considerations apply to any large, complex project, and the appropriate answer depends very much on individual organisational circumstances.

It would certainly be a mistake to define the scope too narrowly. While it may appear, on the surface, that this is a route to quick and easy certification, it is, in fact, a route to a worthless certificate. Any external party, assessing the nature of an organisation's ISMS, will want to be sure that all the critical functions that may affect its relationship are included and a limited scope will not do this. We are aware that some certification organisations are prepared to consider scopes that cover less than a complete business unit; in our opinion, they are doing a disservice to their clients, as well as to the integrity of the ISO 27001 scheme. Do not be tempted by such certification bodies to pursue an approach that is likely to be inadequate to your long-term needs.

The other issue with regard to scope – and that directly relates to the risk management aspects of the project, as well as the project in general – is how it maps onto management responsibilities at the top level. The scope of the ISMS should be aligned with the boundaries of a single management team's responsibility. This should be the management team that has authority to sign the information security policy and has responsibility for directing and managing the organisation that falls within the scope. This means that when it comes to deciding on the acceptable level of risk it is just one person, or group (e.g. board or management team) who decide, and this is demonstrated by one individual signing off the relevant documentation. Of course, it also helps with the smooth progress of the project in general when all those who will contribute fall within the remit of one, dedicated management team.

The overall issue of scoping is certainly one where experienced, professional support can be helpful in assessing the best way forward.

CHAPTER 7: THE ISO 27001 RISK ASSESSMENT

We've already looked at the ISO 27001 risk assessment in the context of the ERM framework and in relation to the PDCA process model. This chapter provides an overview of the steps that ISO 27001 specifically requires, identifies some gaps, and introduces the additional best-practice guidance available in ISO 27002, ISO 27005 and BS 7799-3.[37]

We want to remind readers, at this point, that there is an important difference between a specification and a code of practice. A specification, such as ISO 27001, sets out specific requirements that, if followed, will allow a management system to receive a third-party certificate of conformity. A code of practice, such as ISO 27002, ISO 27005 or BS 7799-3, provides guidance on best practice, but sets out no specific requirements against which a management system can be audited. It is not possible, therefore, for there to be a certificate of conformance with a code of practice.

ISO 27001 contains a specification for the key steps in a risk assessment. Organisations seeking accredited certification to ISO 27001 must – as a minimum – follow these steps. There are no other options. This is not a code of practice – it is a specification, a statement of requirements. You can do more than ISO 27001 specifies and, in some areas, you'll find that you need to – but you must, at the very least, do what is required.

---

[37] BS 7799-3:2017 *Information Security Management Systems – Part 3: Guidelines for information security risk management.*

A code of practice does provide useful guidance. It is not mandatory to follow the guidance, but there is some sense in taking advantage of work that has already been done in order to achieve better results, more quickly. You should remember, though, that whatever guidance you might turn to, no matter how useful it appears, it is the Standard itself that counts. No matter what other experts, or even this book, suggest, it is ISO 27001 itself that defines the one and only set of requirements that need to be met in order to develop and deploy an ISMS capable of accredited certification. The auditor should always turn to a copy of ISO 27001 first and last in order to confirm what its requirements are.

ISO 27002, ISO 27005 and BS 7799-3 are codes of practice. ISO 27002 primarily provides best-practice guidance on the implementation of the 114 controls that are in Annex A of ISO 27001, but it does also provide limited guidance on risk assessment, some of which is useful in developing a risk assessment methodology. ISO 27005 and BS 7799-3, on the other hand, deal specifically with risk assessment and are sensible sources of additional information and guidance on areas in which ISO 27001 is silent, but on which decisions will be required if the ISMS is to work in detail.

Overview of the risk assessment process

As has been mentioned several times, it is important to remember that the risk assessment is part of a larger system, which is the ISMS. Clauses 6.1.1 and 8.1 establish this clearly by providing the context for the risk assessment and linking it to the need to assess risks to the ISMS achieving its objectives ("ensure the information security management system can achieve its intended outcomes"). This is crucial because there is no specific step in Clauses 6.1.2, 6.1.3, 8.2

or 8.3 that will otherwise determine threats specific to these objectives.

ISO 27001 says that the organisation must "define and apply an information security risk assessment process that [...] establishes and maintains information security risk criteria" (Clause 6.1.2). These criteria are two-fold: criteria for risk acceptance and criteria under which a risk assessment will be performed. This will all be established within the context provided by the information security policy, so the organisation must identify a suitable risk assessment methodology that takes into account identified business, information security, legal and regulatory requirements (Clauses 4.2 – 4.3).

ISO 27001 provides no guidance as to how an acceptable level of risk should be defined.

While it is crystal clear on the steps that are required in the risk assessment, ISO 27001 also provides no guidance as to what risk assessment methodology should be adopted. Regardless, the Standard is clear: the criteria against which risks should be evaluated should be established before the risk assessment is undertaken.

ISO 27001 says that the organisation's risk assessment methodology (which should reflect the organisation's risk appetite and/or sit within the existing ERM structure, as we discussed earlier and as required by Clause 5.1) must produce "consistent, valid and comparable results" (Clause 6.1.2 b). This means that once the first risk assessment has been done, any subsequent risk assessments can be compared to it as a baseline or benchmark. As a consequence of this, once controls have been applied in the light of the risk treatment decision, the risk assessment could be repeated and the remaining, residual risks could be confirmed as being within the organisation's level of risk tolerance and that, therefore, the ISMS is effective and the information security policy objectives are being achieved.

Once the risk assessment methodology has been defined, work can get under way. The precise risk assessment steps are that the organisation:

1. Identifies the information security risks (6.1.2 c);

2. Identifies the specific risks associated with the loss of confidentiality, integrity and availability for information assets within the scope of the ISMS (6.1.2 c 1);

3. Identifies owners for each of the risks (6.1.2 c 2);

4. Analyses the impacts that losses of confidentiality, integrity and availability may have (6.1.2 d 1);

5. Assesses the 'realistic likelihood' of these risks occurring (6.1.2 d 2);

6. Determines the level of risk posed by each (6.1.2 d 3);

7. Evaluates the information security risks by comparing the level of risk with the risk acceptance criteria (6.1.2 e 1); and

8. Prioritises the risks for treatment (6.1.2 e 2).

This calculation of the level of risk – what we call the 'risk equation' and which we discuss below – is achieved by first assessing the business, legal/regulatory and contractual impacts on the organisation of security failures (taking into account the consequences of a loss of confidentiality, integrity or availability), then assessing the realistic likelihood of the failure occurring for the given threats and vulnerabilities and (where appropriate) the controls currently implemented.

It assumes that there is an estimable likelihood that an identified threat will exploit an identified vulnerability; if it does, there will be an estimable impact and the product of impact and likelihood gives rise to the risk level. Whether or not that level of risk is acceptable depends entirely on the organisation's risk acceptance criteria.

Clause 6.1.2 e of ISO 27001 then requires the organisation to determine which of these risks are acceptable and which require treatment in light of the criteria set out at the start of the process (6.1.2 a).

The Standard then requires you to "select appropriate information security risk treatment options" (6.1.3 a), and ISO 27000:2018 provides a number of possible headline options for this treatment that BS 7799-3 then boils down to four functional approaches (Clause 8.2):

1. Avoid the risk entirely by either not starting the activity that will lead to it or by ending that activity.

2. Modify the likelihood that the risk will occur.

3. Modify the severity of the risk's consequences.

4. Modify both likelihood and impact.

In a practical sense, methods to achieve these fall into four categories. These are in line with our description in an earlier chapter and are to:

1. Knowingly accept the risks, providing they satisfy the organisation's policies and risk acceptance criteria, i.e. they are within its level of risk tolerance or risk appetite;

2. Modify the risk by applying appropriate controls (treating the risk) to reduce the risk to an acceptable level;

3. Avoid or reject the risks, by, for example, finding a workaround; or

4. Share the business risks with other parties.

The risks that require treatment through the application of controls (option 2, above) are then handled in accordance with Clause 6.1.3 of ISO 27001. Clause 9 of ISO 27005 and Clause 8 of BS 7799-3 provide guidance in this regard. In particular, BS 7799-3 states that controls should be selected on the basis of "the nature and components of the risk(s) that are to be mitigated, the identification of the control objectives that are most appropriate to deliver the desired mitigation and the controls that contribute to the identified control objective(s)". Controls act to reduce likelihood and/or impact, and the objective of the control selection process is to select controls that will bring the identified risk below the previously defined level of risk tolerance, as shown in the risk treatment matrix in Figure 8.

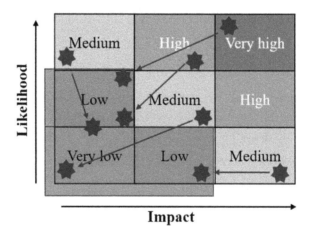

Figure 8: Controls reduce impact and/or likelihood to bring the risk down to the level of risk tolerance/acceptance

The final step in the 'plan' stage of the initial ISO 27001 PDCA cycle is the production of an SoA and a risk treatment plan.

The SoA is the list of all the controls the organisation has selected along with an explanation for their selection and whether or not they have been implemented, and a list of any controls identified in Annex A of ISO 27001 that have not been selected and an explanation why.

The risk treatment plan is the documentation that explains how the controls to be implemented are prioritised in order to manage risk. ISO 27005 advises that priorities can be "established using various techniques, including risk ranking and cost-benefit analysis".[38]

Formal management approval is then required for the SoA, for the proposed residual risks, and for the implementation of the selected controls and operation of the ISMS.

Let's now take a more detailed look at each of the key stages in the risk assessment process.

---

[38] ISO 27005, Clause 9.1.

CHAPTER 8: INFORMATION ASSETS

This chapter will be of greater relevance to organisations pursuing an asset-based risk assessment methodology. While risks do not need to be assessed wholly on the basis of the assets that they threaten, it remains a popular and effective method of risk assessment. Furthermore, for organisations undertaking a scenario-based risk assessment, BS 7799-3 provides the following clarification of the role of asset management:

> Using the scenario-based method does not mean that Annex A control A.8.1.1 is unnecessary. It just means that the asset inventory might not be an input into the risk assessment, whereas Annex A control A.8.1.1 might still be an output of the risk treatment process (i.e. determined by the organization as being a necessary control).[39]

Having said this, the information security policy and the scoping statement discussed in chapter 6 describe the boundaries of the ISMS, and you already have to consider, at a reasonably high level, the information assets that underpin the organisation's business processes in order to establish the scope of the ISMS. You now return to the subject, but this time the objective is to identify all those assets "at a suitable level of detail that provides sufficient information for the risk assessment".[40]

---

[39] BS 7799-3:2017, Clause 7.3.5.
[40] ISO 27005:2018, Clause 8.2.2.

Assets within the scope

For an asset-based risk assessment, the first step is to identify all the information assets (and 'assets' includes information systems – which should be so defined in your information security policy) within the scope of the ISMS and, at the same time, to document which individual and/or department 'owns' the asset. We discuss, in chapter 11, the valuation of assets, particularly in relation to their business, legal/regulatory and contractual requirements.

This asset identification exercise can only take place once the scope – discussed in chapter 6 – has been finalised.

Asset classes

It can be useful to consider information assets in terms of 'classes' or categories. A key benefit of establishing such distinctions is that it allows you to examine how information is managed and used without the distractions of the substance of the information. Such a position is extremely valuable when determining the scope of any ISMS and for identifying assets affected by non-specific threats. We identify, below, six asset classes, which include the asset types we discussed in chapter 6 and should frame your asset identification exercise. They are as follows:

Information assets: this category includes information printed or written on paper, transmitted by post, shown in films, or spoken in conversation, as well as information stored electronically on servers, website(s), extranet(s), intranet(s), PCs, laptops, mobile phones and PDAs, as well as on CD-ROMs, floppy disks, USB sticks, backup tapes and any other digital or magnetic media, and information transmitted electronically by any means. It includes databases and data files, contracts and agreements, system documentation, research information, user manuals, training material, operational or support procedures, business continuity plans, fallback arrangements, audit trails, and archived information.

Software: which includes the sets of instructions that tell the system(s) how to manipulate information (i.e. the software: operating systems, applications, development tools, utilities, etc.).

Physical assets and hardware on which the information is manipulated: such as the computer and communications equipment (including, for instance, laptops, mobile phones, PDAs, etc.), removable media (e.g. USB sticks, CD-ROMs, backup tapes, etc.) and infrastructure assets, such as server rooms, copper cables and fibre circuits.

Services on which computer systems depend: computing and communications services, and general utilities such as heating, lighting, power and air-conditioning (burglar alarms might also be included).

People: who carry a great deal of information in their heads, and the qualifications, skills and experience that are necessary for their interaction with the organisation's data.

Intangibles: such as intellectual property, reputation, brand image, etc.

There should be a link between this inventory and the organisation's fixed-asset ledger and/or its configuration management database (CMDB), and the sensitivity classification (such as that described in ISO 27001 Annex A Clause 8.2) of every asset, together with details of its owner, which should be recorded as well.

A simple exercise is to analyse the information assets that are contained on the average workstation or laptop. These are likely to include, apart from the hardware itself (and, possibly, various peripheral hardware items such as keyboards, mice, etc.), the operating system, individual applications such as email software, word processing and spreadsheet software, and a number of other specific applications, as well as databases, customer records, other contact records, copies of important information, files, folders, email databases, and so on. Each of these assets may have a different classification level, and not all of the assets will necessarily be owned by the user of the workstation.

The objective of the corporate asset identification exercise is to analyse assets down to the level of granularity suggested by the exercise. A usual starting point is with the key corporate information systems or bodies of information. A system consists of a number of components. A single data asset (such as a file, whether electronic or paper) is a component of a system.

These systems will include a number of IT systems (e.g. client relationship management system, payroll system, email system, resource planning system, accounting system, etc.), the telecommunications systems and the paperwork filing systems. The risk analysis team should list the key systems throughout the organisation; there are software tools (for network mapping and software asset management, for instance) that can be used to ensure that all the data assets and all the IT systems have been identified. It might be necessary to deploy software tools to identify all the hardware and software that actually make up the corporate infrastructure.

Telecommunications systems might include mobile phones as well as desk-based systems; personal digital assistants are as important a component of the IT system as are the remote access points and sub-contracted services.

The human resources filing system is as important as that used in the chief executive's or chairman's office. All systems need to be identified and if, in the process of doing this, there is found to be significant sharing of assets or information sharing that was not identified earlier, then the scope of the ISMS may need to be revisited.

Grouping of assets

In most circumstances, it will be beneficial to group individual items and to treat that group as the 'asset' for the purposes of risk assessment. BS 7799-3 says: "it is often unnecessary to calculate risk for each and every asset individually. If several have identical characteristics using the chosen method, then it might be possible to treat them together" (Clause 7.2.3). The key is to ensure that the aggregation of assets into groups does not override the benefit of identifying threats and vulnerabilities at an individual asset level. For instance, it would not be helpful to aggregate all operating systems if the organisation's operating systems include multiple versions of Windows (e.g. Windows Server 2012 R2, Windows 8 and Windows 10) together with Linux and/or Unix, because the vulnerabilities – and therefore the threats – are likely to be different for each. Conversely, looking at all installations of Windows 8 together may be a sensible aggregation.

ISO 27002, 8.1.2 identifies another such circumstance:

> In complex information systems, it may be useful to designate groups of assets which act together to provide a

particular service. In this case the owner of this service is accountable for the delivery of the service, including the operation of its assets.

Asset dependencies

In some cases, the dependency of one asset on another might affect the valuation of both assets and these dependencies should be identified during this phase of the project. For instance, if the integrity of data output from a program depends on the integrity of the data input, then the value of the second depends on that of the first. The integrity of the data might also be dependent on the availability of the power supply and the air conditioning. The confidentiality requirements of a specific data asset might require other assets, in which it is manipulated or stored, to be protected to a higher degree than might otherwise be the case.

ISO 27005 provides helpful guidance here[41]:

- if the values of the dependent assets (e.g. data) are lower than or equal to the value of the asset on which it depends (e.g. software), then its value remains the same;

- if the values of the dependent asset (e.g. data) is greater, then the value of the asset considered (e.g. software) should be increased according to:

  o the degree of dependency, and
  o the values of the other assets.

---

[41] ISO 27005:2018, Annex B, Clause B2.5.

Asset owners

Every asset must have an owner and this is reflected in Annex A control A.8.1.2 (Ownership of assets). In this instance, the term 'owner' doesn't convey legal ownership of the asset to the individual and is defined as the individual or entity "responsible for the proper management of an asset over the whole asset lifecycle". This could, therefore, be a system administrator or a manager who is responsible for defining how an asset or group of similar assets is used.

The owner of the asset is the person – or part of the business – responsible for appropriate classification and protection of the asset. In real terms, allocating ownership to a part of the organisation can be ineffective, unless that part has a clearly defined line of responsibility and individual accountability in place.

It is important to recognise that there may be a number of assets that have users, or custodians, who are not the nominated owners of the asset: for instance, the operating system is likely to be owned by the system administrator, but it will be deployed on workstations throughout the organisation and will be used by workstation users. The system administrator will be responsible for the security (which, remember, includes availability as well as confidentiality and integrity) whereas the users are not accountable for these aspects. It may well be that, as a result of the risk assessment, specific controls (e.g. user access agreements) are imposed on the users.

Sensitivity classification

The asset owner is also responsible for determining the sensitivity classification of the asset. Control A.8.2.1 requires every information asset to be "classified in terms of legal requirements, value, criticality and sensitivity to unauthorised disclosure or modification". While there are comprehensive descriptions[42] of how such guidelines should be developed and applied, there needs to be a direct relationship between the allocated sensitivity classification of an asset and the impact of its security being breached. We discuss impact valuations in chapter 11 of this book. As a general guide, those assets that have a high impact valuation are likely to have a high sensitivity classification, although other factors may also need to be considered.

The key point to note here is that, early in the risk assessment (and, if you are using a risk assessment tool, early in the tool set-up process), you will need to define your classification guidelines and ensure that asset owners are adequately trained to apply both the guidelines and any related asset labelling scheme developed to meet the requirements of control A.8.2.2 (Labelling of information) or similar controls.

Are vendors assets?

We identified one of the classes of information assets as "*Services* on which computer systems depend: computing and communications services, and general utilities such as heating, lighting, power and air-conditioning". This gives rise to a simple question: are the suppliers/vendors of these essential services also assets?

There are two practical answers to this question. The best solution is probably to use a mix of the two, but in doing so

---

[42] See, specifically, chapter 9 of *IT Governance: An International Guide to Data Security and ISO27001/ISO27002*, Alan Calder and Steve G Watkins (Kogan Page, 2019).

it is essential that the exact approach to be used in each specific case is determined by a common set of rules. These should be defined in the risk assessment documentation.

One option is to decide that the vendor itself is not an asset – the organisation that is within the scope of the ISMS does not own the vendors – but that the services provided by the vendor and, possibly, the relationship with the vendor are both assets within the scope of the ISMS. The logic behind this option is that a relationship with a vendor can be an asset if it is a key supplier in terms of the information aspects of whatever it is they supply.

For example, a stationery supplier would not, we suggest, be a key relationship for the purposes of information security (even if you argue that without pencils you cannot write, since you can easily go and buy pencils from someone else). On the other hand, if you have invested a lot of time and effort (and hence money) in selecting, educating and building a relationship with a specific supplier, then that relationship has value to you and is therefore, by definition, an asset.

A word of warning, however: it is advisable to set clear criteria for including suppliers in or excluding them from the risk assessment process or the process will become unmanageable. So, if it is relatively easy and cost-free to find an alternative provider for any one vendor, without compromise of confidentiality, integrity or availability, then we suggest the relationship is excluded from the asset register. You might like to set some figures for 'relatively easy and cost-free' so that all asset owners apply the criteria consistently when deciding to include/exclude a supplier.

For example, the service provided by a disaster recovery (DR) company is an asset. A contractual relationship with a

DR company is part of a control that brings identified risks within an acceptable tolerance, and, therefore, has value to your company – you pay for it, so it must have.

Vendors, however, bring a whole host of threats with them and these may well provide the context for how you accommodate them in your risk assessment methodology. For instance, it may be necessary to consider the threat to other assets of vendors not doing exactly as you might want.

The second approach to vendors is, therefore, to consider them – or rather the danger of them not – providing what you require, as a threat. For example, if you have a bespoke piece of software developed by a one-person contractor, the danger is that the one person or source of expertise to service the software becomes unavailable one way or another. This threat could exploit the vulnerability that the software may have, e.g. code weaknesses or requires regular maintenance, and you should be able to determine the likelihood of the asset being compromised in this way. The impact is determined by the value of the asset to the business; consequently, the risk can be determined.

What about duplicate copies and backups?

Security breaches in respect of duplicate or backup copies will not necessarily have the same impacts as they would in respect of the originals. Duplicates are usually kept in different media or environments, and are subject to different threats from the originals. The impact on the organisation of compromise in respect of a copy might be the same as, less than or more than the original.

For instance, destruction of a backup copy of an exchange folder will not have the same impact on information availability as would destruction of the original – *unless* the original was already unavailable. Conversely, data confidentiality may be more easily compromised if off-premise backup tapes are attacked than if the servers are threatened. The duplicate copy of an asset must, in other words, be assessed as an asset in its own right.

An alternative approach – more suited to paper copies and digital duplicates of information assets – is to treat the existence of duplicate copies as vulnerabilities in the security of the original asset. The logic is that a photocopy, or an e-copy, will contain all the information that is in the original, but will be beyond the security perimeter devised for the original. The existence of the copy is, therefore, a vulnerability in respect of the original; one logical control is to disable all copying capability.

There is a relevant sub-question in relation to backups, which concerns the security of the various information assets that are backed up to a single source.

Backups should be considered a specific asset. Backups are kept and generated in order to mitigate a specific risk, but the backups themselves face risks, either the same ones as the original assets they back up and/or different ones, but those risks have to be identified and mitigated. With regard to the ISMS and the information risk assessment, you can treat a backup tape (say) as one asset, even though it contains duplicates of many separate assets. This makes sense as any controls applied to the backup will typically be applied to the whole, rather than sub-sections of it. Yes, it contains many assets, all of which have their own classification and impact value, but the challenge of assessing backups of each and every asset separately would be impractical and would add no real value.

The important thing to remember is that when applying controls relating to confidentiality to the individual assets that are backed up, the same degree of restriction should be applied to that part of the backup media on which they are stored – and, where a backup contains assets of varying sensitivity, the classification level appropriate to the most sensitive should be applied to all.

Identification of existing controls

ISO 27001 says that the risk assessment must take account of existing controls. This means that you need to identify the controls that are in place at the point you commence your risk assessment. You do this, as ISO 27005 points out, to "avoid unnecessary work or cost, e.g. in the duplication of controls" (8.2.4), and recommends that this step should be carried out at the time of identifying the assets. This makes sense: you will find it useful to have to hand information about existing controls as you start considering threats and vulnerabilities. Information about existing controls should be included with the asset information; sensible risk assessment tools will enable you to gather this information in a format that reflects the controls contained in Annex A of ISO 27001.

CHAPTER 9: THREATS AND VULNERABILITIES

The second step in the asset-based risk assessment process is to identify the threats to the identified assets. The third step is to identify the vulnerabilities those threats might exploit. Threats and vulnerabilities go together and, for that reason, we are addressing them together in this chapter.

The difference between 'threats' and 'vulnerabilities' is not always immediately clear to people new to the subject and, as a risk assessment process is implemented within an organisation, it will not be immediately clear to everyone involved in it. It is very important to always differentiate clearly between these two attributes of a risk, because the existence of the risk itself is dependent on the coexistence of a threat and a vulnerability.

The simple difference is this:

- Vulnerabilities are flaws or weaknesses in an asset.

- Threats can accidentally trigger or intentionally exploit a vulnerability to compromise some aspect of the asset.

The first thing to remember is that there are very many threats that have absolutely no relevance to many organisations. A simplistic example would be an organisation that has no Internet connectivity: it can be blithely unconcerned with the huge array of Internet-based threats, because there is no vector that those threats can exploit to attack the network and, therefore, it has no exposure to them.

The moment that it connects to the Internet, it does need to be concerned; the point of connection is by definition a possible point of vulnerability and, therefore, an area where controls might be required. As we shall see later, control selection should depend on the organisation's assessment of the likelihood and potential impact of specific Internet threats and should be focused on trying either to reduce the level of the threat or to reduce the extent of the vulnerability.

Threats, in other words, are external to information assets, and vulnerabilities are typically attributes of the asset – aspects of the asset that the threat can exploit. While threats tend to be external to the assets, they are not necessarily external to the organisation. The majority of information security incidents today originate within the organisation's secure perimeter.

The range of threats includes: hostile outsiders, such as criminal hackers, non-hostile outsiders, such as suppliers or cleaning contractors, and insiders, both the disaffected and the committed, but also the careless or just the poorly trained. Vulnerabilities are security weaknesses in the existing systems, which can either be exploited by threats or which allow damage, accidental or otherwise, to information assets.

For example, dropping a laptop is a threat to the asset (the laptop), and the vulnerability exploited by that could be the lack of robustness in the laptop's design. Similarly, a liquid spillage may be a threat to a laptop and the vulnerability would be its lack of keyboard waterproofing.

For each of the assets within the scope of the ISMS, it is necessary to identify the potential threats and the possible vulnerabilities. The essential relationship, from an information security point of view, between threats and vulnerabilities leads us to think of them as 'combinations'. We're not concerned with either threats or vulnerabilities on their own, but with them in combination. We therefore speak of 'threat-vulnerability combinations'. There are a number of threat-vulnerability combinations that apply to any one asset, and any one threat typically may have more than one vulnerability that it can exploit. It should also be noted that a threat to one asset is not necessarily a threat to another. For example, a fire in the server room is a threat to a number of systems based there, but is unlikely to be a threat to an organisation's externally hosted mobile phone network.

There are very many threats and the range of possible vulnerabilities is also substantial. Examples of threats and vulnerabilities are contained in ISO 27005, BS 7799-3 and NIST SP 800-30. Threat and vulnerability databases are increasingly widely available, and any good risk assessment tool should contain both.

Some threat-vulnerability combinations will be unique to specific industries, which may lead to the introduction of controls additional to those in ISO 27001 Annex A. Many of the threats and their related vulnerabilities will also be technical in nature. Technical vulnerabilities need special treatment, and these are further discussed below.

Threats

As we've said, threats are things that can go wrong or that can 'attack' the identified assets. They can be either external or internal. Examples might include fire or fraud, virus or worm, criminal hacker or terrorist. Threats are always present for every system or asset: because it is valuable to its owner, it will be valuable to someone else. You could assume that, if you cannot identify a threat to an asset, that it is not really an asset. So the next stage is to identify the potential threats to the systems and assets listed in compliance with A.8.1.1, and identified in the previous chapter.

Essentially, threats for each of the systems should be considered under the following headings:

- Threats to confidentiality

- Threats to integrity

- Threats to availability

These categories are in line with the ISO 27001 requirement to identify risks to those same characteristics.[43]

Some threats will fall under one heading only, others under more than one. It is important to have carried out this analysis systematically and comprehensively, to ensure that no threats are ignored or missed. The quality of the controls that the organisation eventually implements will reflect the quality of this exercise, and of the overall risk assessment.

A number of external threats might be classified under all three headings. A criminal hacker might be able to steal confidential data and then disrupt the information system so that data is no longer available or, if it is, it is corrupted. A virus can affect the integrity and availability of data, and, because it could mail out a copy of an address book, confidentiality as well. A business interruption, such as a fire in the server room or a filing cabinet, is initially likely to affect the availability and integrity of information.

So, under this methodology, you identify, on an individual basis, threats to the confidentiality, integrity and availability of every asset within the scope of the ISMS. You can do this through a brainstorming exercise or by using an appropriate

---

[43] ISO 27001:2013, Clause 6.1.2 c) 1.

threat database; technical expertise is essential if the threat identification step is to be carried out properly.

It is, as we've said, likely that an individual threat may appear against a number of assets but, crucially, ISO 27001 requires the ISMS to be erected on the foundation of a detailed identification and assessment of the threats to each individual information asset that is within the scope. From a practical point of view, if a number of assets fall within the same class and are exactly the same (e.g. desktop computers that have the same hardware specifications, software build, connectivity configuration and user exposure), they might be considered a group of assets and the subsequent phases of this exercise could be carried out treating them on that basis. Where there is any doubt or uncertainty, however, resort to assessing threats on an individual asset basis.

Vulnerabilities

Vulnerabilities leave a system open to attack by something that is classified as a threat, or allow an attack to have some success or greater impact. For example, for the external threat of 'fire', a vulnerability could be the presence of inflammable materials (e.g. paper) in the server room. In the language of BS 7799-3, "A threat exploits a vulnerability to compromise the confidentiality, integrity and/or availability of an item of information".[44]

The next stage in the assessment process, therefore, is to identify – for every single one of the assets that you have identified and for each of the threats that you have listed alongside each of the assets – the vulnerabilities that each

---

[44] BS 7799-3, Clause 7.2.3.

threat could exploit. Clearly, a single asset could face a number of threats, and each threat could exploit more than one vulnerability.

A common question is: should we identify vulnerabilities with or without those controls that are currently in place? Does the fact, for instance, that we have a firewall mean that we do not have a vulnerability to hacking attacks?

The correct answer is that you should do both. You should identify the vulnerability that would be exploited by the threat if you didn't have any controls in place, because you want to assure yourself that those controls that are in place are appropriate for the identified risks (in some cases, implemented controls are in excess of those identified as actually required in the light of the assessed risks and the organisation's risk appetite). You also want to identify the controls that are currently in place, and you want to be in a position to identify any residual risk (see chapter 14), in order to consider whether or not additional controls may be required. Those controls that are already in place will be operated as part of the organisation's ISMS and the confirmation that they are appropriate controls, and are to be retained, must come from the formal risk assessment.

Technical vulnerabilities

Many of the threats related to information technology arise because of technical vulnerabilities. A number of information systems are sold with in-built and widely known vulnerabilities. All wireless (Wi-Fi) products, for example, are designed to communicate 'out of the box' with one another and, therefore, come without any security settings configured. Routers and other access control units come with default password settings that are widely known. All software has imperfections, and the more complex the software, the more imperfections it will have. Each imperfection is a potential vulnerability. CVE[45] identifies tens of thousands of unique, standardised names of vulnerabilities and security weaknesses. Bugtraq[46] has more than 3,000 pages listing publicly known software vulnerabilities, across all operating systems and applications.

Attacks are often devised to exploit specific vulnerabilities.[47] An increasing number of attacks are launched before patches are available, and exploit code for many of the most popular attacks is commonly available on the Internet. Many attacks are automated and indiscriminate (geographically, sectorally and size-wise) in their target selection. Integrity and availability of data are, often, more likely to be compromised by these threat-vulnerability combinations than is confidentiality. The SANS CIS Critical Security Controls[48] is a list of the most critical controls on the basis of the most popular current attacks on information systems.

Your risk assessment should not, however, attempt to individually identify every single one of these threat-vulnerability combinations – there are too many of them. New ones constantly appear while old ones continually evolve. What you *should* do is identify the generic threat

---

[45] CVE, the Common Vulnerabilities and Exposures dictionary, is at *http://cve.mitre.org*.

[46] Bugtraq is at *www.securityfocus.com/vulnerabilities*.

[47] There is a description of malware in *IT Governance: An International Guide to Data Security and ISO27001/ISO27002*, Alan Calder and Steve G Watkins (Kogan Page, 2019); that book also deals with criminal hackers and their motivations.

[48] Published by the SANS Institute, at *www.sans.org/critical-security-controls*.

(hacking, malicious code or malware) and the generic vulnerability (software weaknesses), with a generically high likelihood and a medium or high impact.

The control that you would apply is the generic control A.12.6.1 (Management of technical vulnerabilities). The baseline implementation of this control should be to ensure that all controls identified in the SANS Critical Security Controls are implemented in order to mitigate a vast swathe of common vulnerabilities. Thereafter, appropriate external vulnerability or penetration tests should be run on a regular basis (weekly, monthly or quarterly – depending on your risk assessment) to identify whether or not newly identified vulnerabilities have appeared in the software deployed on your network, and these should be patched to a priority determined by their risk.

Today's combination attacks and the growing use of ransomware suggest that external vulnerability testing should be combined with phishing and social engineering awareness training in order to secure the human element of your operations against becoming a vector for cyber threats that sidestep common technological defences.

CHAPTER 10: SCENARIO-BASED RISK ASSESSMENT

While asset-based risk assessment is a perfectly valid approach to risk assessment, it is not the only method, nor is it necessarily the best or the easiest. For some organisations, an asset-based risk assessment may be unnecessarily detailed, too time-consuming, or simply unfeasible for the specific risks that the organisation faces.

You should note, however, that BS 7799-3 does not favour one method over the other and, in fact, considers them fundamentally identical, stating:

> An event is the action of a threat exploiting a vulnerability. [...] The consequence is the result of the event [...] which in the asset-threat-vulnerability method is the asset and the nature of the compromise. In this sense, both methods are identical.[49]

Scenario-based risk assessment is based on the premise that, instead of examining the threats and vulnerabilities affecting a specific asset or class of assets, the risk assessor can instead identify the scenarios that could compromise information security and determine the impact and likelihood of those scenarios coming to fruition. For instance, one organisation might look at its paper records and identify flooding as a risk to the integrity and availability of those records (an asset-based approach), while another will simply identify flooding as a risk and then determine the possible consequences, which may include the integrity and availability of paper

---

[49] BS 7799-3:2017, Clause 7.3.1.

records, as well as the availability of computer systems that are unable to operate while flood waters inundate the ground floor, building access, etc. (scenario-based approach).

BS 7799-3:2017 covers scenario-based risk assessments in quite a lot of detail, specifically clarifying that "risks can be identified and assessed through an evaluation of events and consequences" (Clause 7.2.2). This is quite a different approach, but will still need some method of determining the consequences, such as by understanding the value of the individual assets as will be described in the next chapter.

ISO 27000 provides a useful set of definitions for 'event' (as distinct from 'information security event'), beginning by stating that it is an "occurrence or change of a particular set of circumstances" (Clause 3.21). This provides important information: an event could be the consequence itself of another event – a knock-on event, which we discuss below. In a note, ISO 27000 clarifies that "An event can be one or more occurrences, and can have several causes", and, furthermore, that "An event can consist of something not happening". So some events can be the result of complex interactions – and thus potentially difficult to identify or predict – and others could be the result of plans failing to complete or opportunities failing to materialise.

'Knock-on' events are those that arise from other events – they are part of another event's consequences. For instance, an event might reduce the organisation's access to its security logs, which means that the organisation cannot use that information to identify or react to another event. Alternatively, an event might create other vulnerabilities or lead very directly into another event. While it might be sensible to treat both events as a single scenario, the consequences may be better dealt with if treated as separate events. This will depend entirely on the organisation's appreciation for the risks posed by each event.

For many organisations, it may be a trivial process to identify the general scenarios that could occur – theft, cyber attack, natural disasters, and so on.

Scenarios – or events – can be identified using a couple of techniques:

1. Identify events that apply to any comparable organisation.

2. Identify events specific to the organisation.

The first of these is supported by databases of events and indicative consequences, and benefits from external expertise – consultants, perhaps, who have conducted a number of risk assessments for comparable businesses. The second is provided by internal expertise and analysis.

BS 7799-3 describes a method for tracking events and the nature of the consequences in order to provide a quick reference for the risk treatment plan; for example:

Event	Consequence			Comments
	C	I	A	
Power surge	-	Y	Y	-
Hacking	Y	Y	Y	Treat DoS of public-facing servers as separate event
Disclosure	Y	-	-	All forms of disclosure not included in other events

For this method, the aim is not to perform a completely thorough and granular risk assessment but to quickly identify all the controls necessary to protect the organisation and its assets. Because many events have similar characteristics, treating one risk will often mitigate the risk posed by another.

This method allows the organisation to quickly identify major concerns and logically determine their impacts. It provides a quick, effective method of dealing with major risks and those that are readily understood, especially to those who are outside the process. A table such as that above should be simple enough for anyone to understand, regardless of their familiarity with risk management, which can make it a valuable tool for communicating risks at all levels of the organisation.

On the other hand, the obvious lack of detail and granularity makes it simple to overlook less immediate risks. This is compounded when determining the consequences (impact) because it is equally easy to overlook the harm to specific assets if they are not the subject of the assessment.

The theft of mobile devices, for example, might identify consequences for confidentiality and availability, but it may not recognise that one class of mobile device often contains significantly more valuable data and that the consequences of loss or theft would, therefore, be commensurately greater. Equally, another class of mobile device – a tablet taken to trade shows, for instance – might be largely devoid of any valuable information, so ordinary controls to protect information are excessive.

With this additional information, the organisation might – quite reasonably – choose to apply additional or stronger controls in order to mitigate the risk, or clarify the situation by considering them different events. Aside from relying on asset owners and internal expertise to identify specific scenarios worthy of attention, a solution might be to cross-check the assessment with a prioritised asset register to ensure risks are treated appropriately.

In any case, the consequences of an event will need to be evaluated, in which case a general assessment may suffice (e.g. the organisation expects a certain event to cause damages within a certain range) or a blended approach can be taken whereby the assessment attempts to identify the impact on the classes of information assets that might be affected.

CHAPTER 11: IMPACT, INCLUDING ASSET VALUATION

Risk assessment involves identifying the potential business harm that might result from a risk coming to fruition. The way to do this is to assess the extent of the possible loss to the business for each potential concern. One object of this exercise is to prioritise treatment (controls) and to do so in the context of the organisation's acceptable risk threshold, so it makes sense to categorise possible loss in terms of impact on the organisation of the risk occurring.

The successful exploitation of a vulnerability by a threat will have an impact on the asset's confidentiality, integrity or availability. This may have consequences for the business, in terms of its actual operations, or from a compliance angle, or in relation to a contractual requirement. A single threat could exploit more than one vulnerability and each exploitation could have more than one type of impact. These impacts should all be identified.

Impacts

Clause 6.1.2 of ISO 27001 requires that the organisation "identify risks associated with the loss of confidentiality, integrity and availability", and that it "analyses the information security risks [to] assess the potential consequences that would result if the risks [...] were to materialize". ISO 27001 also requires that the organisation "establishes and maintains information security risk criteria that include [...] the risk acceptance criteria". It provides *no guidance* as to how those criteria should be developed other than suggesting (via reference to Clauses 4.1 and 4.2) that the whole risk assessment process should consider the organisation's context and the needs and expectations of interested parties.

Furthermore, ISO 27001 provides *no guidance* as to the basis on which control selection decisions should be made, other than to say that they should be selected "taking account of the risk assessment results" (6.1.3 a), which will necessarily take into account how the organisation prioritises the risks for treatment (6.1.2 e.2).

Finally, the ISO 27001 management system clauses have *no requirement* in terms of your methodology for the identification or valuation of information assets.

How you value an asset in an asset-based methodology is, however, going to be fundamental to how much you will be prepared to invest in protecting it. ISO 27000 doesn't offer a definition for an asset, although it is reasonable to simply define it as 'anything that has value to the organisation'. The organisation's fixed-asset register is unlikely to provide practical help in this regard: many critical assets may already (through application of the financial depreciation policy, or of the accounting convention that assets should be shown on the balance sheet at the *lower* of historic cost – less depreciation – or current market value) have been written down below their actual useful value to the organisation. Many other, even more critical, assets (such as brand value, key supplier and customer contracts, staff know-how, intellectual property and databases) may not even be on the fixed-asset register at all. Many of these assets may even have a current market value in excess of the historic cost and, in some cases, this value appreciates over time, rather than depreciates.

Resolution of these issues is fundamental to the development of an ISMS that will meet the requirements of ISO 27001; you must have clearly defined criteria that enable management to knowingly and objectively accept risks as a decision clearly distinct from choosing to treat or avoid risks. These criteria must reflect some practical relationship between the potential impact of an information asset-related threat on the organisation and the level of investment that will be made to prevent that happening.

These issues are, therefore, fundamental components of the organisation's risk assessment methodology. As we said earlier, the Standard requires the organisation to identify risks and the impacts that losses of confidentiality, integrity and availability might have.

Furthermore, the results of the risk assessment must be used to inform the correct ascription of controls, which may be determined in light of the value of each asset (i.e. the importance of the asset to the organisation, or the impact on the organisation that would result from a compromise of each of confidentiality, integrity and availability) and the threats and vulnerabilities that, in combination, make up the likelihood of the asset being compromised. Equally, it could be on the basis of the value of assets likely to be compromised as the result of a given event.

The Standard is clear that the consequence of confidentiality, integrity and availability being compromised needs to be considered. Depending on the scale, complexity and context of the ISMS these factors could be considered together, or separately. Addressing them together better suits a relatively small, low-risk environment whereas considering them separately is more appropriate in a larger organisation where the risk considerations are likely to be considered in a more granular manner and the risk treatment plan will detail the different controls to preserve confidentiality (e.g. encryption) and availability (e.g. backups) separately. This consequence, whether confidentiality, integrity and availability are combined or addressed separately, should take into account business, legal/regulatory and contractual implications.

Defining impact

BS 7799-3 recommends (and ISO 27005 concurs) that impact values "should take into account the wider consequences that might result" (Clause 6.4.2), and then lists a range of possible types of harm, including loss of life or harm to individuals or groups, damage to public trust, impaired operations and breaches of contracts or service levels, in addition to the more obvious immediate financial harm. ISO 27001 is concerned primarily with negative impacts, to be described in terms of loss or degradation of the confidentiality, integrity or availability of an asset.

Confidentiality is lost when information suffers unauthorised disclosure. 'Unauthorised' ranges from breach of data protection or privacy legislation, to breach of contractual requirements, to betrayal of commercially or personally sensitive data.

Integrity is lost when unauthorised changes are made to information or information assets, whether accidentally or deliberately. Failure to repair losses of integrity can lead to further corruption and integrity loss in other information assets.

Availability is undermined when those (people or systems) authorised to access information in order to do their jobs are unable to do so or suffer delay.

This means that it can be beneficial for each asset to be valued separately for each of confidentiality, integrity and availability as the controls prescribed to safeguard each aspect are likely to be different. You should, therefore, identify one by one the likely impacts for each threat-vulnerability or event-consequence combination within the scope of your ISMS, and for each of confidentiality, integrity and availability.

This has to be taken further. Every information asset is, as we have seen, likely to be affected by at least one threat-vulnerability combination or by an event's consequences. Every such incident might compromise each of the confidentiality, integrity and availability of the asset, which means that you may have to make three yes/no decisions. For each of the three information attributes, there may be an impact that has business consequences, one that has legal/regulatory consequences, and one that has contractual consequences. You must therefore assess, for each of these possibilities, what that impact might be. You have, in other words, potentially nine decision points in respect of each threat-vulnerability or event-consequence combination for each information asset.

Here's an example using a threat-vulnerability assessment:

Imagine the risk assessment carried out in relation to an organisation's unencrypted backup tape, and specifically how it is transported to secure off-site storage. A threat – driver forgetfulness or inattention – might exploit a vulnerability – the van door doesn't close properly unless it is forced shut and locked – with the consequence that the backup tape might fall out into the road while in transit. There is a realistic likelihood of this happening, and the potential impacts can be assessed as follows:

Confidentiality of the information on the backup tape will be compromised; the business's reputation for protecting its customer data will be undermined and it will lose a quantifiable level of revenue; there will be legal consequences, which can also be quantified, arising from the breach of the privacy of the individuals whose data is on the tape; and there will be contractual consequences arising from the breach in specific customer contracts that require protection of their data.

Integrity of the backup tape may be compromised because the tape may be damaged on falling out of the van while it is in transit; this will have a business impact when it proves impossible to restore the most recent version of a specific user document that has been corrupted in error; it may have a legal consequence when a later court case is unable to access a critical document for which no other copies exist; and it may have contractual consequences if the tape contains data that has to be surrendered to the customer on completion of the contract.

Availability of the backup tape will be compromised; the business impact may be an inability to continue operations when faced with a business continuity event and this will have quantifiable consequences; the legal consequence may be that the directors are prosecuted for their failure to be adequately prepared to protect the company's assets; the contractual consequences may include a breach of a customer contractual requirement for effective backup processes.

While methodologies do exist that, having determined individual values for these impacts, add or multiply them together to try to reduce the actual risk assessment workload, practical experience demonstrates that the results produced by these methodologies skew the risk treatment decisions. For instance, an asset with a very high confidentiality impact level and a very low availability impact level needs different controls for risks to confidentiality than to availability. Should you apply controls that are more appropriate for one risk than the other, or should you apply something 'in the middle' that is appropriate for neither? In either case, what you have is a situation in which your risk treatment decision is not directly related to the risk, and the investment in the controls is unlikely to be in proportion to the potential impact against which you are guarding. In other words, this sort of approach is unlikely to lead either to an ISMS that conforms to ISO 27001 or to one that is cost-effectively optimised.

The risk analysis above doesn't yet include an assessment as to the actual cost of the impact on the organisation in any of the nine identified areas, nor does it include an assessment as to the likelihood of occurrence of the threat-vulnerability combination. It is, therefore, impossible to determine which of the identified risks should be accepted, which rejected and which transferred or controlled.

Estimating impact

Part of how we make that decision has to take into account the cost of controlling the risk: should we spend more, less than, or the same as the potential cost of the impact?

ISO 27001 defines the purpose of an ISMS as "[preserving] the confidentiality, integrity and availability of information by applying a risk management process and [giving] confidence to interested parties that risks are adequately managed" (Clause 0.1). ISO 27002 expands on the role of risk management in Clause 0.3. It says:

The selection of controls is dependent upon organizational decisions based on the criteria for risk acceptance, risk treatment options and the general risk management approach applied to the organization, and should also be subject to all relevant national and international legislation and regulations. Control selection also depends on the manner in which controls interact to provide defence in depth.

This is helpful guidance, in that it says "impact is estimated", not "quantifying cost", of risks, and about "organizational decisions" in relation to security controls. This guidance, which is in line with a qualitative risk assessment methodology, is a particularly helpful starting point for considering impact value.

BS 7799-3 takes this guidance still further: it says that an asset can be valued "depending upon its classification, the more sensitive or more important the information, the higher the value, or in relation to the consequence(s) of it being compromised [...] Moreover, the value of the asset might depend on the nature of the compromise: an asset low in sensitivity could have a high requirement for accuracy and availability" (Clause 7.2.3). The value of the asset should, in simple terms, be the same as the impact value of compromising it.

Our earlier analysis of the threat-vulnerability combinations that might compromise a backup tape is in line with the view that assets should have more than one value. As mentioned earlier, BS 7799-3 confirms this view by recommending that "the organization should take into account the wider consequences that might result", and suggests that a standard asset valuation scale should be defined for assets to help asset owners correctly value their assets.

11: Impact, including asset valuation

BS 7799-3 recommends creating an impact valuation scale to guide asset owners and risk assessors in their valuation activity. The starting point for creating such a scale is to estimate the possible cost of impact. One traditional method (one that we recommend, and which is also contained in both ISO 27005 and BS 7799-3) of estimating impact is to identify, value and aggregate all the direct (e.g. legal) and indirect (e.g. brand diminution) costs of an event, all the costs of recovery, repair, rectification and (possibly) lost opportunities and lost revenue. The resulting total cost of (potential) loss is the impact value.

A stepped set of impact levels (e.g. high-medium-low) can then be designed that reflects the ranges of estimated impact, such that, for instance, all impacts with an estimated cost between £15,000 and £150,000 might be classified as 'medium'. These levels should be appropriate to the size of the organisation, its appetite for risk and its current risk treatment framework. They should be approved by management, as part of its approval of the overall risk management framework.

While it is true that, in reality, there will be variations between the actual impact of different risks, there is no value in calculating these variations precisely: the range within which the impact value of similar risks might fall is such that the same control decisions are likely to be made in respect of each. A qualitative methodology, which enables you to look at similar risk levels as though they were the same, is cost-effective and produces comparable and reproducible results.

You should note that, although you are using monetary values to make the boundary levels comprehensible to assessors, the reason for this is to ensure that they are able to produce comparable results, rather than to apply a quantitative methodology, which this is not.

Your risk assessment approach should, therefore, ask you to input impact values separately for each of confidentiality, integrity and availability. More than that, it should follow BS 7799-3, ISO 27005 and the methodology we outline here. Use impact values as the asset values.

The starting point in asset-based impact assessment is to identify the 'owner' (as described in ISO 27001 Annex A control A.8.1.2): the person who decides how the asset is used, by whom and for what purpose. The owner is best placed to explain and evaluate the damage done to the organisation if the asset's confidentiality, integrity or availability is compromised. The asset owner should consider what business processes the asset supports, as well as the legal and contractual requirements in terms of the asset, and derive from these the value of the asset in terms of the cost to the organisation of compromise to each of the asset's three information security attributes: confidentiality, integrity and availability.

When valuing each asset, the key question is: 'What value does this attribute of this asset have to the organisation and what would it cost us if it were compromised?' The fixed-asset register valuation and the financial cost of replacement are at best likely to be minor contributors to this exercise, which is far more based on a qualitative assessment of value.

The scale of this exercise is substantial. It is extremely difficult to carry out manually, requiring an excessive commitment of resources. It may also involve an assessment methodology that contains a high level of subjectivity, as a result of which the methodology is likely to fall foul of ISO 27001's "consistent, valid and comparable" requirement.

The only way that the risk assessment can be done cost-effectively, in terms of resource deployment and process accuracy, is by using an appropriate risk assessment tool.

The asset valuation table

We've said that the organisation would find an asset valuation table useful to guide risk assessors in assigning values to information assets within the scope of the ISMS. We have already seen that the risk assessment needs to produce reproducible and comparable results, and consistency in asset valuation is essential to this.

We also summed up current guidance on the approach to asset valuation by pointing to BS 7799-3 guidance that says that assets should be valued to take into account "the wider consequence that might result [from] breaches of legal, regulatory or statutory requirements" (Clause 6.4.2) and that "Events and consequences can often be determined by a discovery of the concerns of top management, risk owners and the requirements identified in determining the context of the organisation" (Clause 7.2.2). Clearly, the asset value is not the original cost of acquisition, nor is it the cost of replacement – although these aspects should be included in the impact valuation.

In a qualitative methodology, we need an appropriate asset valuation scale to support this process. You could use something like that shown in Table 1.

Table 1: Asset Valuation Table

Asset value → ↓ Security attribute	Low	Medium	High
Confidentiality	Impact is less than £15,000	Impact £15,000 – £149,000	Impact in excess of £150,000
Integrity	Impact is less than £15,000	Impact £15,000 – £149,000	Impact in excess of £150,000
Availability	Impact is less than £15,000	Impact £15,000 – £149,000	Impact in excess of £150,000

In this table, the impact in each instance is the total cost of impact, including reputational damage, which itself is briefly discussed later in this chapter.

The impact evaluation should include, as part of this total cost of loss:

- Monetary loss;

- Productivity loss (which relates to the role of the asset in business processes);

- Loss of customer confidence; and

- Reputational damage.

It also needs to take into account:

- Objective(s) of process(es);

- Criticality of process(es) to the business and business objectives; and

- Information sensitivity.

Business, legal and contractual impact values

Your risk assessment methodology can use as the impact value the highest of confidentiality, integrity and availability values, or a sum of them, or to carry out the assessment separately for each attribute of each asset. The third is usually the most sensible approach, as many controls are designed to deal with security issues around one – but not all – of the three information security attributes.

You should also remember that ISO 27001 requires the risk assessment to take into account the business, legal, regulatory and contractual requirements for information security; it is entirely possible that, in respect of an individual asset, there will be different requirements and, therefore, different values in each of these areas.

For instance, a police force must keep personal data confidential so that it can comply with the Data Protection Act, but it may also need to ensure that the information is available to other police forces investigating a crime (business need). A healthcare provider will have a contractual responsibility to keep patient information confidential, a business requirement to maintain the integrity of that information (for instance, keeping the medical history up to date) and a compliance requirement to protect that data from exposure. The potential impacts of a breach of security in each of these areas could be different.

You therefore have to consider how the information is actually used in the organisation – in other words, in the context of the business, legal and regulatory, and contractual requirements for information security – before you can really make an informed decision about the most appropriate approach to pursue.

Your methodology must be sufficiently practical to actually work, and a fully ISO 27001-compliant risk assessment tool should simplify risk assessments being made for each information security attribute for each of business, legal and contractual requirements.

Reputational damage

Reputational damage – a major concern of boardrooms and shareholders – is likely to be an impact of most breaches of information security. It can, however, be very hard to incorporate into a risk assessment process where the results need to be "consistent, valid and comparable".

Again, the solution for this challenge can be as simple or as complicated as you want to make it. We recommend using one of the two following approaches:

1. **Direct description approach**
   The direct approach is one where the asset owners use an agreed customisation of the table that follows (Table 2) to determine the contribution that reputational damage would have on the impact value for that (attribute or component of that) asset for risk assessment purposes.
2. **Coverage approach**
   An alternative approach, in which the contribution of reputational damage to the value of the asset is estimated in light of the adverse coverage that might result, could use a customised version of Table 3. Each entry in the level of impact column would be given a value, which

would be used in helping to determine which impact band in Table 1 the value of the asset falls into.

Of course, those organisations that do not have a reputation to protect will not need to factor in this aspect of impact; for those that do, the input of the organisation's PR advisers may be particularly useful.

Table 2: Direct Impact of Reputational Damage

Description of impact of reputational damage	Contribution to impact value of asset
Likely to jeopardise existence of organisation	£££££££££££ £££££££££££
Likely to jeopardise ability to function in one sector and/or geographical area (continent or country)	££££££ ££££££
Likely to result in law suit directly related to core competence	££££
Likely to result in law suit not directly related to core competence	££
Likely to jeopardise relationship with one or more existing high-worth clients	££
Likely to create ill-feeling in one or more high-worth clients	£
Likely to jeopardise relationship with five or more low-worth clients	¾ £
Likely to create ill-feeling with more than one low-worth client	½ £
Likely to create ill-feeling with one low-worth client	¼ £

Table 3: Coverage Impact of Reputational Damage

Contribution to impact value of asset	Media coverage			Specific client level
	TV	Press	Radio	
£££££££££££ ££££££	National	National	National	–
£££££££££££ ££	Regional	National	National	–
£££££££££££	Regional	Regional	National	–
£££££££££	–	National	Regional	–
££££££££	–	Local	Regional	–
££££££	–	Local	Local	–
££££	–	–	Local	–
££££££££	–	–	–	Jeopardise reputation with one sector
££££	–	–	–	Damage reputation with one major client that jeopardises current and future contracts
££	–	–	–	Damage reputation with one major client that jeopardises future contracts

CHAPTER 12: LIKELIHOOD

Each of the preceding stages of the risk assessment has a relatively high degree of certainty about it. The vulnerabilities should be capable of technical, logical or physical identification. The way threats might exploit them should also be mechanically demonstrable. Defined scenarios have predictable consequences. The decisions that have to be made are those that relate to the actions the organisation will take to counter those threats. Before that, however, there needs to be an assessment as to the likelihood of the event, and what the appropriate response to it will be. This means that the actual risks have now to be assessed and related to the organisation's overall 'risk appetite' – that is, its willingness to take risks.

Risk analysis

ISO 27001 (Clause 6.1.2 d) sets out the requirements in terms of analysing the risks. Until this point, the assessment has been carried out as though there was an equal likelihood of every identified threat actually happening. This is not really the case and this is, therefore, where there must be an assessment – for every identified impact – of the likelihood or probability of it actually occurring. 'Likelihood' in the risk equation is a value representing the probability of an identified threat exploiting a specific vulnerability in the asset.

Probabilities might range from 'not very likely' (e.g. major earthquake in Southern England destroying primary and backup facilities) to 'almost daily' (e.g. several hundred automated malware and hack attacks against the network).

Again, a simple set of stepped, qualitative levels should be used.

The likelihood level should be estimated by considering the frequency at which the threat is likely to occur in the future and the probability of the threat exploiting and/or breaching the vulnerability when it does occur:

Likelihood = Frequency of threat occurring x Probability of vulnerability being breached

Most methodologies simply make, for each identified threat, a single assessment as to the likelihood of the threat occurring and exploiting the vulnerability, or the event happening, and then map that level directly to the estimated impact level in order to arrive at an assessed risk level.

For threat-vulnerability-asset assessments, some methodologies insert an intermediate step, which involves a matrix that helps calculate the likelihood level by reference to the probability of both the threat occurring and the probability of it successfully exploiting the identified vulnerability.

For example, an intermediate likelihood matrix constructed on that basis might look like the one in Figure 9.

In this example, using three-level scales for each of the vulnerability and threat frequency axes gives a five-level (very low – low – medium – high – very high) likelihood scale. Of course, the boundaries for each of the scales for the threat and vulnerability axes need to be defined so that the assessment results can be reproduced and will be comparable.

High	Medium	High	Very high
Medium	Low	Medium	High
Low	Very	Low	Medium
	Low	Medium	High

(Probability of vulnerability breach — vertical axis)

Frequency of threat occurrence

Figure 9: Likelihood matrix

Either approach is acceptable for the ISO 27001 risk assessment. As long as the method for determining likelihood is defined so that it can be estimated in a manner that supports a consistent, valid and comparable information security risk methodology, the process will satisfy the requirements of the Standard. The decision as to whether or not there should be an intermediate step is one entirely for the organisation.

Information to support assessments

For the risk assessment methodology to provide "consistent, valid and comparable results", there certainly needs to be some objective basis of guidance for assessing or estimating likelihood.

A key challenge is that, while risk assessment may draw substantially on historic records, risk management decisions are based primarily on assessments of the future. While one can – and should – use history (and that means collecting, analysing and improving detailed monitoring statistics) in order to inform one's assessment of the future, it is extremely important to bear in mind that 'things change' and the 'thing' that changes most for today's organisations is the risk environment.

Just because a risk has never turned into an incident to date does not mean that it never will. This may seem an obvious statement, but its implications need to be kept in mind when conducting and reviewing risk assessments. The rate of change in technology alone is, for instance, a key source of risk for enterprises.

Historic data, facts and figures are all, nevertheless, going to be of enormous value in the risk management process. Historic figures about the risk environment (frequency and nature of threats, the cost of successful attacks, the costs of various mitigation measures, and so on) all inform the initial risk assessment, as well as the ongoing risk management process. As we shall see in due course, ISO 27001 expects us to measure the effectiveness of the controls that we select and to use this information to feed the continual improvement process.

There are a number of challenges in creating this data, including:

- Defining a robust methodology that enables the process and outcome to be consistent, valid and comparable, for estimating costs, such as reputational damage, the inadvertent disclosure of confidential information, and disaster recovery costs;

- Evaluating control implementation costs, and particularly their impact on productivity;

- The rate of change in threats, technology/vulnerabilities and control options/tools to address them; and

- Ascribing values and likelihoods to potential future events, in an environment that is more likely to bring new threats than to repeat old ones.

It will be essential that the risk management process has built into it sub-processes for collecting relevant information about threats and activities undertaken and, particularly, about changes in the risk environment, so that management can use this information to improve and strengthen its ISMS.

CHAPTER 13: RISK LEVEL

Risk level – the output of the risk equation that we discussed earlier – is a function of impact and likelihood (probability). The final step in the risk assessment exercise is to assess the risk level for each impact and to transfer the details to the corporate asset inventory.

Three levels of risk assessment are usually adequate: low, medium and high. Where the likely impact is low and the probability is also low, then the risk level could be considered very low. Where the impact is at least high and the probability is also at least high, then the risk level might (depending on the design of the risk matrix) be either high or very high.

Every organisation has to decide for itself what it wants to set as the thresholds for categorising each potential impact, and from time to time it may be helpful to have four or more risk levels (including one such as minimal) in order to better prioritise actions.

The risk scale

The basic risk scale, which is set out in Figure 10, plots estimated impact against estimated likelihood.

In this scale, a different category of labels has been applied to both the impact (lower-case alphabetic characters) and the likelihood (lower-case Roman numerals) scales to indicate low, medium and high. The reason for doing this is to avoid confusion in discussions and communications between members of the risk assessment team and with other parties. For example, a high likelihood (iii) and a high impact (c) identify something that would be very high risk, whereas a medium risk in the table is a function of likelihood (i) and impact (c), or (ii) and (b), or (iii) and (a).

High	c	Medium	High	Very high
Impact	b	Low	Medium	High
Low	a	Very low	Low	Medium
		i	ii	iii
		Low	Likelihood	*High*

Figure 10: The risk scale

While that is clear, the table only becomes useful when each band has objective criteria applied to it that enable different people in different parts of the organisation to use it on a consistent basis.

The usual way of doing this is to allocate specific ranges to each band. For instance, the impact bands might be:

a   From £0 to £99,999

b   From £100,000 to £999,999

c   From £1 million to £5 million (anything in excess of £5 million is rejected)

The likelihood bands might be:

i   Less than once every year (very infrequent)

ii   Between once a month and once a year (often)

iii More than once a month (very often)

These bands enable different people, in different parts of the organisation, to assess risks in a similar way. Automated hacking attacks on an online bank, for instance, would be placed in impact category b (between £100,000 and £999,999) and likelihood category iii (very often); the assessed risk level would therefore be 'high'. Similarly, manual hack attacks might be placed in impact level c (more than £1 million) but only at likelihood level ii (often). Intersection of these two lines would also give rise to an assessed risk of 'high'.

The qualitative methodology has been useful in enabling different risks to be quickly assessed, and for comparative risk assessment decisions to be made – without detailed, faux-accurate calculations as to potential impact.

Both risks fall outside the organisation's risk tolerance level, and both should be controlled. The organisation's risk acceptance criteria include the requirement that the cost of control should be in line with the identified potential impact. But how do we determine, in this example, how much to spend on implementation?

Boundary calculations

One approach is to calculate the risk value (risk = impact x likelihood) at the borders of each risk value and for the investment criteria to be as simple as: spend no less than [the lower risk level] and no more than [the higher risk level]. Each level has an upper and a lower boundary, the point at which the risk shifts from being at one level to being at the next. For example, the border values for 'very low' in our table would be:

Lower boundary: a (low) x i (low), or 0 x 0, which equals zero.

Upper boundary: a (high) x i (high), or 1 x £99,999, which equals £99,999.

In other words, according to this risk assessment scale, this risk would have an impact that falls somewhere between £0 and £99,999 and the risk treatment decision (if this risk was outside the risk acceptance boundary) would allow no more than £99,999 to be invested in control implementation.

While this appears clear cut, the situation is less clear for those risk levels that occur more than once. For instance, the medium risk level (let's call it risk 1 in this example) could fall within the ranges of:

Impact high (c) and likelihood low (i), the boundaries of which would be:

Lower boundary: c (low) x i (low), or £1 million x 0, which equals 0.

Upper boundary: c (high) x i (high), or £5 million x 1, which equals £5 million.

The medium risk level also exists at the intersection of impact (b) and likelihood (ii). The boundary calculations (for what we will call risk 2 in this example) would be:

Lower boundary: b (low) x ii (low), or £100,000 x 1, which is £100,000.

Upper boundary: b (high) x ii (high), or £999,999 x 12, which is (about) £12 million.

So, a risk (risk 1), assessed as a medium risk, has a potential impact of between £0 and £5 million. Another risk (risk 2), also assessed as a medium risk, has a potential impact of between £100,000 and £12 million. These clearly different impact ranges need to be recognised when developing the organisational risk assessment methodology, and there are three useful ways of responding to them.

1. The first is to ensure that the scale you use is sufficiently granular; in real terms, a five-level scale may – for many organisations – provide a more useful basis of assessment.

2. The second is for the risk assessment methodology to explicitly recognise that there will be 'fuzzy boundaries' to the risk levels, and for the board to delegate authority to the risk assessor to review and adjust (what we call 'smoothing') those individual control decisions that appear to be misaligned as a result of these calculations, to ensure that there is an equivalence of investment.

3. The third is to use 'mid-points' instead of boundary calculations to provide guidance on control investment. While these calculations do not remove the need to address both points 1 and 2 above, they do reduce the magnitude of the overlap and, therefore, can provide more useful risk assessment guidance.

Mid-point calculations

Calculating the mid-points for each range can guide investment decisions.

The starting point for this calculation is to identify mid-points (i.e. the points between the upper and lower levels) for each of the risk factors (likelihood and impact). The mid-points for each of the factors in Figure 14 would be:

| Ia | = £50,000 | Li = | 0.5 (times a year) |
| Ib | = £500,000 | Lii = | 6 (times a year) |

Ic   = £5 million   Liii =   52 (times a year)

We can then apply these to calculate the mid-point for each of the identified risks, to produce what we call a 'risk value indicator'. Please note the term 'indicator': we are using a qualitative methodology, and this is an indicator to provide guidance.

Risk Level		Risk value indicator	
Very high	=Liii x Ic	=52 x £2.5m	= £130m/yr
High	= Liii x Ib	= 52 x £500k	= £26m/yr
	= Lii x Ic	= 6 x £5m	= £30m/yr
Medium	= Liii x Ia	= 52 x £50k	= £2.6m/yr
	= Lii x Ib	= 6 x £500k	= £3.0m/yr
	= Li x Ic	= 0.5 x £5m	= £2.5m/yr
Low	= Lii x Ia	= 6 x £50k	= £300k/yr
	= Li x Ib	= 0.5 x £500k	= £250k/yr
Very low	= Li x Ia	= 0.5 x £50k	= £25k/yr

As these calculations demonstrate, there is a range of risk value indicators for each risk level, even when considering only the mid-point in the corresponding likelihood and impact scales. From an investment perspective, the control investment decision will be to invest an amount approximately the same as the risk value indicator. As guidance goes, the risk assessment team will find this more useful than guidance based on boundary calculations. It is well worth remembering here the 'approximately correct rather than precisely wrong' mantra.

The organisation's documented risk acceptance criteria should, if a mid-point calculation is used, include a description of how it is calculated and how the risk value indicator is to be used in risk treatment decisions. The formal risk acceptance criteria should also state that, while it is the mid-points that have been used to demonstrate the different levels of risk and guide control investment decisions, it is the entire level that is either within or outside the acceptance criteria.

CHAPTER 14: RISK TREATMENT AND THE SELECTION OF CONTROLS

Once you have completed the risk assessment, you can move on to the selection of controls. This chapter reviews the requirements of ISO 27001 around control selection, which is also known as 'risk treatment'.

As we said in chapter 1, there are four risk treatment decisions that can be made:

1. Avoid/reject the risk by deciding not to pursue the practices and/or arrangements that give rise to the risk.

2. Retain/take the risk, keeping it under review.

3. Modify/reduce risks to 'acceptable' levels through the application of controls.

4. Share the risk with another party, whether through contract or insurance.

The criterion that is used in making the decision is simple: either the risk is within the risk tolerance level, in which case it is accepted, or it is not, in which case it must be avoided, modified or shared. So, in principle (unless the risk is too great):

If risk level < risk acceptance criteria, then 'accept' risk; or

If risk level > risk acceptance criteria, then 'modify' risk (which can include share), or if extreme consider avoiding it.

If the risk is too great (i.e. the potential impact is off the scale, or is greater than the 'very high' level chosen in the risk assessment methodology), then the risk must be avoided, which might involve implementing some form of 'workaround' in order to do so. A simple example of this response to a risk assessment might be where the potential impact of theft of equipment from the offices of a company would be so great if it moved to a particular neighbourhood that it decided against the move.

Types of controls

Controls are the countermeasures or safeguards designed to reduce risks, and are applied to reduce the likelihood of something happening or of its impact if it were to happen. There are three types of control that are commonly applied to reduce the risk:

1. Preventive controls protect vulnerabilities and make an attack unsuccessful or reduce its impact.

2. Detective controls discover attacks and trigger preventive or reactive controls.

3. Reactive controls reduce the impact of an attack and/or help with recovery after an attack.

Control types can fall into four different categories:

1. Technical controls, which usually involve system configurations, software packages and network issues.

2. Organisational controls, which relate to direction, guidelines, policies and procedures put in place by management.

3. Physical controls, which deal with day-to-day issues such as physical security and environmental concerns.

4. People; controls related to personnel.

As we indicated in chapter 3, it is essential that the controls that are implemented are cost-effective. The principle is that the cost of implementing and maintaining a control should be no greater than the cost of the impact at the identified frequency, and this principle should be written into the board-approved risk acceptance criteria contained in the information security policy.

There are also practical considerations that should be kept in mind when selecting controls:

- Likely effectiveness of the recommended control.
- Legislation and regulatory requirements (both for and against).
- Organisational policy.
- Operational impact (is the control likely to have a negative effect on the operational capacity of resources?).
- Safety and reliability.

ISO 27005 identifies some additional constraints that should be considered when selecting controls[50]:

Time constraints: controls should be capable of being implemented within an acceptable timescale, in relation to both the lifetime of the system and the period of exposure to the risk.

Financial constraints: controls should be implemented within the set budget and the constraints of the cost-benefit analysis.

---

[50] ISO 27005:2018, Clause 9.2 and Annex F.

Technical constraints: issues such as the compatibility of programs, software and hardware have to be taken into account.

Operational constraints: controls should be built into designs right from the start.

Cultural constraints: the active support of staff for a control is usually essential, so if staff do not understand or support a control decision, it is unlikely to be effective.

Ethical constraints: these are often tied into legal requirements, such as privacy and data protection, and may be more applicable to some industries than others (e.g. healthcare).

Environmental constraints: space availability, climatic conditions, geography, and so on can all influence the selection of controls.

Ease of use: controls should be selected for optimal ease of use while achieving acceptable residual risk to the organisation.

Personnel constraints: the necessary expertise can be expensive, difficult to source or otherwise limit the range of controls that can be selected.

Constraints of integrating new and existing controls: new controls may be limited by or hinder existing controls.

It is not possible to provide total security against every single risk. It *is* possible to provide effective security against most risks, but the risks can change and so the process of reviewing and assessing risks and controls is an essential, ongoing one.

Clause 6.1.3 of ISO 27001 requires the organisation to select appropriate controls, and requires this selection to be justified. While it is implicit that the organisation will select these from the reference list in Annex A of ISO 27001, this is not a strict requirement.

It may be that the organisation needs, in the light of its risk assessment, to implement controls other than those listed in Annex A. It might, for instance, have specialist processes that require additional security measures, or highly sensitive equipment that needs added protection. Additional controls can be added to the 114 that are already listed in Annex A. It would be sensible for an organisation that is adding controls to choose them from a reputable source (and to document the reasons for the choice), such as the hardware or software vendor (e.g. Microsoft or Cisco), NIST,[51] the ISF,[52] COBIT®[53] or some other source of good-practice guidance.

Regardless of the source, ISO 27001 invites organisations to approach this exhaustively and says, quite clearly, that the organisation must compare the controls that it selects against the reference controls in Annex A. This process ensures that the organisation considers whether or not a set of broadly applicable controls or control objectives are necessary to treat its risks.

ISO 27001 auditors are likely to challenge implemented controls that are in excess of those required by the risk assessment on the basis that this may indicate inadequate

---

[51] The US National Institute of Standards and Technology has a specialist Computer Security Resource Center with many highly important information security resources: *http://csrc.nist.gov*.

[52] The Information Security Forum is a private, members-only group with high membership fees, at: *www.securityforum.org*.

[53] Control Objectives for Information and Related Technology, available from ISACA®: *www.isaca.org*.

controls applied elsewhere. ISO 27002:2013 provides implementation guidance for each of the controls listed in Annex A of ISO 27001:2013 (although note that it is the organisation's risk treatment plan that will indicate how a control is to be implemented for any given risk/asset(s)). There are, however, some areas in which organisations may need to go further than is specified in either standard, and the extent to which this may be necessary is driven by the extent to which technology and threats have evolved since the publication of both standards.

BS 7799-3 advises selecting controls in the light of a control objective, stating that "The determination of controls should be informed by the nature and components of the risk(s) that are to be mitigated, the identification of the control objectives that are most appropriate to deliver the desired mitigation and the controls that contribute to the identified control objective(s)" (Clause 8.2). A control objective is a statement of an organisation's intent to control some part of its processes or assets and what it intends to achieve through application of the control. The cost of implementing (in cash and resource deployment) each control should not exceed the potential impact (assessed in line with the guidance in chapter 6) of the risks (including safety, personal information, legal and regulatory obligations, image and reputation) it is designed to reduce.

It is important that, when considering controls, the likely security incidents that need to be detected should be considered and planned for. In effect, the process of selecting individual controls from those listed in Annex A should also include consideration of what evidence – measures of effectiveness – will be required "to provide information on whether the information security management system is effectively implemented and maintained"[54] and that each risk has been reduced to an acceptable level. In other words, controls must be constructed in such a manner that any error, or failure during their execution, can be promptly detected and that planned corrective action, whether automated or manual, is effective in reducing the risk of whatever may happen next to an acceptable level.

Annex A of ISO 27001 has 14 major categories of control, each of which has a number of subsections. There are 114 sub-clauses, each of which has a four-character alpha-numeric clause number. Each of these is a control under ISO 27001 and each needs to be considered and a decision made as to whether or not it is applicable. The outcome of that decision is recorded in the SoA, which is described in the next chapter.

The application of a control should reduce the risk it is designed to address. It will not always reduce that risk below the acceptable risk level. In this case, additional controls must be selected and applied until the cumulative effect of the controls is to reduce the identified risk below that acceptable risk threshold. The principle of not investing more on controlling a risk continues to apply as the size of the risk is reduced by the application of successive controls. It is, in other words, worth remembering that each additional control that is applied, is applied to a reduced risk level and that, therefore, it would be inappropriate to invest as much in the subsequent controls as in the initial one.

---

[54] ISO 27001:2013, Clause 9.2.

Risk assessment and existing controls

The risk assessment should assess the realistic likelihood of security failures occurring in the light of the controls currently implemented. While this is obviously the correct approach for a second and subsequent risk assessments, it is not terribly helpful in respect of the initial risk assessment, in that it assumes that all the controls that have already been applied – usually without the benefit of a structured risk assessment – are appropriate controls for the identified risk.

In fact, it is quite often the case that organisations discover that some of their controls are in excess of their requirements and can be reduced; the consequent savings benefit the bottom line or enable other controls to be deployed elsewhere. Furthermore, as BS 7799-3 notes, "Factors that affect the likelihood of the occurrence of the event and their consequences of events can change, as can factors that affect the suitability of or cost of the various treatment options" (Clause 12.3), which is echoed by ISO 27005.

The logical approach (which should be reflected in your methodology and, therefore, in your choice of risk assessment tool) is, as we indicated earlier, for the initial risk assessment to take place only after identifying the existing controls. It makes sense, in other words, to identify all existing controls that are applied to each asset or risk at the point of identifying the assets and then carrying out the initial risk assessment, and then potentially do both a 'before' and an 'after' assessment.

You should easily be able to identify, in the 'after' assessment, those risks that you have 'over-controlled' by the fact that, in comparison to the 'before' assessment, the 'after' assessed risk level is very close to zero (i.e. well within the risk acceptance criteria) and where the removal or reduction of controls would not necessarily move the risk out beyond the level of risk tolerance.

This approach will enable you to link your risk treatment plan (see chapter 15) directly to the risk assessment, insofar as you will be able to identify that, for some risks, no further action is necessary whereas, for others, controls will either be implemented or dismantled.

Some refer to risk levels calculated ignoring the effect of any controls that may be in place as the 'gross risk' and those that are estimated in light of the prescribed controls as 'net risk'. Note that the SoA should identify the controls required by the 'before' assessment and should, therefore, reflect all the controls applied.

Residual risk

Whatever risk is left after some controls have been applied is known as 'residual risk' – the residual risk will vary as more controls are implemented, or the effectiveness of existing controls varies over time. In most cases, the residual risk achieved once all of the prescribed controls have been implemented will be below the acceptable threshold and, therefore, obtaining the risk owner's approval (prior to implementation) should be a formality, assuming the timescale to achieve this is acceptable.

There will be circumstances where it has not been possible to reduce risk below the acceptable level (where, for instance, the cost of implementing an appropriate control is much greater than the impact value of the remaining risk that is outside the risk tolerance level) and this residual risk must also be explicitly signed off as acceptable by the risk owner.

Risks can, as we've said, never be reduced to zero, even with the largest security budget. The possibility that one of the attributes of information security (i.e. confidentiality, integrity and availability) will be compromised will always exist. Prescribing additional measures will, of course, incur extra cost and offer diminishing returns in terms of increased information security. This is where the fourth option for treating information security risks comes in.

Risk sharing

Most organisations will at least consider sharing some of the risk or, rather, reducing the impact of some risks by transferring them to a third party, such as through insurance. While there are other methods of sharing risk, almost all of them rely on one form of contractual agreement or another – contracting a specific process to an organisation better able to handle the risk, for instance, or requiring a supplier to assume responsibility for the risk. Insurance is certainly the most popular method of risk transfer. The aim here is to limit the potential financial losses by obtaining protective cover at a reasonable cost.

Insurance can be purchased to cover most risks. It is vital to ensure that any insurance you purchase matches the exact needs and risks identified. Buying inadequate cover, whether an inappropriate amount or for the wrong circumstance, will leave an unacceptable level of residual risk that may only be identified when it is too late.

In addition to the traditional insurance policies, specialised policies addressing information security risks are becoming more widely available. Underwriters can be found for all types of insurance needs, with sufficient shopping around.[55]

Marrying suitable arrangements to transfer risks with risk control and avoidance policies can provide a risk strategy that meets organisational needs. Suitable implementation and monitoring result in a residual risk that reflects the organisation's risk appetite.

Risk sharing, however, is not the same as risk avoidance. When sharing risk, the ultimate accountability for that risk still rests with the transferor. If, for instance, the transferee insurance company refuses to pay, or becomes insolvent, the transferor will still bear the full impact of the risk. It is important, therefore, that the effectiveness of risk sharing strategies is reviewed on a regular basis; risk transfer policies should be subject to testing in just the same way as are business continuity plans.

Optimising the solution

There is a lot of benefit to preparing a cost-benefit analysis for the risk treatment plan, which itself will be further discussed in chapter 15. A cost-benefit analysis could also be a sensible step in the 'plan' phase for all future control decisions, for proposed new controls or for enhanced controls. It would encompass the following:

1. Determining the impact of implementing the new or enhanced controls.

---

[55] At the time of writing, an international standard, ISO/IEC 27102, is being developed to provide guidance on the adoption of cyber insurance as a risk treatment option.

2. Determining the impact of *not* implementing the new or enhanced controls.

3. Estimating the total costs of the implementation. These should include all those components that your organisation routinely uses to calculate total cost of ownership (TCO) and may include, but are not limited to:

   - Hardware and software purchases;
   - Reduced operational effectiveness if system performance or functionality is reduced as a result of increased security;
   - Cost of implementing additional policies and procedures;
   - Cost of hiring additional personnel to implement proposed policies, procedures or services;
   - Training costs; and
   - Maintenance costs.

A cost-benefit analysis, carried out at the point of selecting controls, enables the organisation to select those controls that will deliver most security enhancement for the lowest total cost, and will provide the basis for driving future improvements through the ISMS.

CHAPTER 15: THE STATEMENT OF APPLICABILITY

Having conducted the risk assessment and taken decisions regarding the treatment of those assessed risks, the results need to be documented. This produces two documents:

1. Statement of Applicability (SoA)

2. Risk treatment plan

The SoA lists all the controls the organisation has selected alongside a justification for their selection and whether or not they have been applied within the ISMS, and also identifies any controls from Annex A that have not been selected along with a justification for their exclusion. The risk treatment plan maps the selected treatments (and the measures by which they are to be implemented) to the specific risks they are intended to address and is, in effect, a control implementation plan; we discuss this further in chapter 16.

Drafting the Statement of Applicability

As the controls are selected, the SoA can start being drawn up. This SoA (specified in Clause 6.1.3 d of ISO 27001) documents the decisions reached on each control in light of the risk assessment and is also an explanation or justification as to why each of the controls that are listed in Annex A have or have not been selected. This exercise, of reviewing the list of controls and documenting the reasons for including/excluding them, is a useful cross-check on the control selection process.

The SoA must be effectively reviewed on a regular basis, as and when the information security risk assessment is reviewed and updated. It is likely to be one of the first documents that an external auditor will want to see. It is also the document that is used to demonstrate to third parties the spread of controls that have been implemented and is referred to, with its issue status, in the certificate of conformity issued by third-party certification bodies.

The SoA could adopt the format set out in the example below, in which the wording provided in the Standard is repeated with appropriate variations to reflect the actual decisions made by the management steering group and its reasoning. The SoA can also refer to other documents, where these form the basis for any specific decisions recorded in it.

There are different ways of expressing how different controls are applied, some of which are shown below. The SoA should be signed by the owner of the security domain for which it has been drawn up. This document is, for the external certification auditor, key evidence of the steps taken between risk assessment and implementation of appropriate controls; it often contains references to the parts of the ISMS that enforce or implement those controls.

Introduction

This is the Statement of Applicability, as specified in Clause 6.1.3 d of ISO 27001:2013 ('the Standard'), for ABC Ltd. It was adopted by the management steering group on [date]. It reflects a risk assessment carried out on [date]. Controls are addressed in the same order and using the same numbering as in Annex A of the Standard, and this statement explains which controls have been adopted, and identifies those that have not been adopted, setting out the reasons for these decisions.

All of the prescribed controls have been implemented unless indicated otherwise.

Statement of Applicability

A.5.1.1 Policies for information security

ABC Ltd approved an information security policy that conforms to the guidance of ISO 27002:2013 on [date], and has published and communicated it to all employees and relevant external parties.

A.5.1.2 Review of the policies for information security

All policies related to information security are reviewed at least annually or when determined necessary by the information security steering group. Reviews are conducted in accordance with ABC Ltd's policy review process.

A.6.1.1 Information security roles and responsibilities

ABC Ltd has established an information security steering group, which reports to the CEO, and which includes representatives from all the key parts of the organisation. This group approved – and is responsible for regular reviews of – the information security policy and is responsible for assigning and/or resourcing security roles within the organisation, and for driving and reviewing implementation across the organisation of the ISMS and any individual initiatives, including information security training and awareness. An external information security adviser has been contracted to provide specialist advice as well as ongoing expertise to the steering group.

[Through all controls, e.g.]

A.8.3.3 Physical media in transit

> This control has not been adopted, as ABC Ltd's physical media never leaves its premises.
>
> [Or]
>
> *A.11.2.1   Equipment siting and protection*
>
> In each situation where there is a possibility that sensitive information might be overseen, a risk assessment is carried out and the appropriate controls, as identified in this section, are applied.

This book does not explore each of the controls specified under Annex A, as those are addressed elsewhere.[56]

The SoA must also list those additional controls that the organisation has determined, following its risk assessment, are necessary. These controls should be listed, either within those control sections whose objectives are supported by the additional controls, or within additional control sections added after those contained in ISO 27001 Annex A. It would also be worth documenting how the additional controls were selected.

It is sometimes argued that an organisation's SoA should not be made available to anyone outside the organisation and, possibly, even subjected to restricted accessibility within it. However, given that the ISO 27001 accredited certificate of conformity will explicitly reference the SoA document and the version number that was current at the most recent

---

[56] See, for instance, *IT Governance: An International Guide to Data Security and ISO27001/ISO27002*, seventh edition, by Alan Calder and Steve G Watkins (Kogan Page, 2019), as well as the various books on the ISO 27001 series from IT Governance Publishing.

certification audit,[57] it is reasonable to expect that those looking to examine the degree of assurance your organisation's ISMS provides will ask to see it. Of course, you could insist on them signing a non-disclosure agreement before letting them see the document. Alternatively, you could classify the document, or at least one version of it, as publicly available, with a different, more comprehensive version containing any sensitive information being given a tighter security classification.

---

[57] It is possible a more recent version was current at the time of the most recent audit: the reference on the certificate would not need updating unless the selection of controls had changed.

CHAPTER 16: THE GAP ANALYSIS AND RISK TREATMENT PLAN

While the SoA identifies which of the ISO 27001 Annex A controls (and which, if any, additional controls) have been selected and the implementation status of each, it does not prioritise implementation or provide any guidance for how implementation is required to be carried out.

Of course, it would be logical for the organisation to tackle and implement controls in the order of priority (i.e. those that address 'very high' risks first). The controls that are most critical for the organisation will be those that relate to the threats and vulnerabilities that it has identified, through the risk assessment process, as being most serious to its most critical systems.

Gap analysis

The reality is that most organisations that set out to achieve ISO 27001 certification already have a number of information security measures in place. In chapter 14 we touched on the requirement to identify and record the original controls when doing the initial risk assessment. ISO 27001 requires that those controls that are in place are adequate and appropriate, and that additional required controls are implemented as quickly as possible. In other words, although the Standard does not explicitly require one, an analysis of the gap between what is in place and what is required following the risk assessment should be carried out.

This gap analysis can be conducted either bottom-up or top-down. A bottom-up analysis will start with the information gathered during the risk assessment process about all controls currently in place, and then assess whether or not they are adequate to meet the requirements of the organisation's SoA and the Standard. A top-down approach starts with the controls identified in the SoA and assesses, by comparison with the existing controls, the extent to which the new requirements have already been met. The authors' preferred approach is the top-down one, as this will most quickly identify the critical holes in the existing security systems, as well as the controls that are unnecessary and can be eliminated or limited.

The SoA will be complete once all the identified risks have been assessed and the applicability of all the identified controls has been considered and documented. Usually, the Statement is started before any controls are implemented and completed as the final control is put in place.

The gap analysis is really the essential step in creating the risk treatment plan and, when compared to the original 'benchmark starting point', can act as a progress report.

Risk treatment plan

Clause 6.1.3 e of the Standard requires the organisation to "formulate an information security risk treatment plan". Risk treatment is, as we saw earlier, part of the risk management process.

There is a link to ISO 27001 Clause 5.1, which is a substantial clause dealing in detail with management responsibility. Clearly, the risk treatment plan needs to be documented. It should be set within the context of the organisation's information security policy and it should clearly identify the organisation's approach to risk and its criteria for accepting risk, as discussed elsewhere in this book. The risk assessment process must be formally defined, and responsibility for carrying it out and reviewing it must be formally allocated. At the heart of this plan is a detailed schedule, which shows for each identified risk – linked either to an asset-threat-vulnerability combination or to a scenario:

- The associated risk level (from the risk assessment tool);

- The gap between the assessed risk and the acceptable level of risk;

- How the organisation has decided to treat the risk (retain, avoid, modify, share);

- The control gap analysis:

  o What controls are already in place and their nature (e.g. detective, preventive, etc.).
  o What additional controls are considered necessary, and their nature (and details of any supporting cost-benefit analysis).

- The resources required for the task (financial, technical and human); and

- The timeframe for implementing the controls.

The risk treatment plan links the risk assessment (contained in the chosen risk assessment tool and its outputs) to the identification and design of appropriate controls, as described in the SoA, such that the board-defined approach to risk is implemented, tested and improved. This plan should also ensure adequate funding and resources for implementation of the selected controls and should set out clearly what these are.

The risk treatment plan should also identify the individual competence and broader training and awareness requirements necessary for its execution and continual improvement.

We see the risk treatment plan as the key document that links both components of the risk management process and continual improvement of the ISMS. It is a high-level, documented identification of who is responsible for delivering which risk management objectives, of how this is to be done, with what resources, and how this is to be assessed and improved; at its core is the detailed schedule describing who is responsible for taking what action, in respect of each risk, to bring it within acceptable levels.

CHAPTER 17: REPEATING AND REVIEWING THE RISK ASSESSMENT

Effective risk management is a continual cycle, which, as described earlier, might be in the mould of the Plan-Do-Check-Act cycle or some other process model. This means, of course, that the risk assessment must be regularly revisited. ISO 27001 sets out the requirement very clearly, requiring management to "review the organization's information security management system at planned intervals", including considering "results of risk assessments and status of [the] risk treatment plan" (Clause 9.3).

In addition to this formal management review, the organisation may need to conduct additional risk assessments to take into account changes in the business environment, to the organisation, to the risks it faces, to the incidents it experiences, to regulatory changes and in the light of the effectiveness of the controls. The need for these further risk assessments will be defined at the beginning of the risk assessment implementation by identifying "criteria for performing information security risk assessments" (Clause 6.1.2 a 2). These criteria might be influenced by changes to the organisation and its business objectives, the risk environment (i.e. threats, vulnerabilities and likelihoods), the emergence of new technology and changing usage of existing systems, and changes to regulatory and compliance requirements.

Following the initial, resource-intensive phase of the 'ISMS implementation' risk assessment, the organisation's appetite to repeat the exercise is likely to have diminished significantly. The real value in having done a comprehensively thorough risk assessment – using a tool that retains the data so that it can support future reviews – is that it enables you to achieve certification *and* you will be able to use it time and time again to review progress and ensure that the residual risk remains exactly where you want it: beneath the risk acceptance criteria.

Given the rate of development of new threats, the discovery of new vulnerabilities and the development of new technology (with its own inherent vulnerabilities), the ISMS needs to be continually reviewed to ensure it remains fit for purpose and that it meets the requirements of the information security policy. To do this, the risk assessment needs to be reviewed.

There are two types of review: a review that takes place in response to a specific change of circumstances, such as a proposal to introduce a new technology, provide a new service or respond to a regulatory change; and a review that takes place on a regular basis and which considers the overall effectiveness of the controls that are currently in place. This regular review should take place at least annually in smaller businesses, but in larger organisations should probably be done on a rolling monthly schedule, which ensures that the entire risk assessment is reviewed across the 12-month period.

Review(s) should be part of the overall management review of the ISMS and should look at the aggregated outputs of the incident reporting procedure as well as from the various processes put in place to measure the effectiveness of controls (as required by Clause 9.1).

The Standard describes the reviewing of the ISMS and risk assessment so as to make sure it continues to satisfactorily manage information security risks as "continual improvement". The real benefit, though, of such a continual improvement process is in the improved economy and effectiveness of the controls that address the identified risks (the latter being used to improve the return on information security investment, and hence, economy again).

The actual process of reviewing the risk assessment can be as straightforward as you wish: at the basic level, this would involve:

- Formalising any changes to the organisation's risk management framework and risk acceptance criteria;
- Identifying any changes to the information assets of the business that hadn't already been recorded for risk assessment purposes;
- Identifying any previously unrecorded changes to the business, regulatory and contractual contexts;
- Identifying any previously unrecorded changes to the risk environment (i.e. new or changed threats, vulnerabilities, likelihoods or impacts);
- Identifying any resultant changes required to the risk treatment and control decisions;
- Identifying any resultant changes to residual risk calculations and, if there is an increase in residual risk, obtaining formal approval for it; and
- Ensuring that the process is fully documented.

APPENDIX 1: vsRISK CLOUD

As we've said in this book, risk assessment is a *core competence* for information security management. We've also said that, without using a database risk assessment tool, it is virtually impossible to adequately manage an ISO 27001-compliant information security risk assessment in any organisation that has more than a handful of staff and very few information assets.

In this book, we have recommended vsRisk Cloud, and our reasons for doing so are contained in chapter 5. This appendix complements that chapter.

If you wish to purchase a copy of vsRisk Cloud, here is a link:

www.vigilantsoftware.co.uk/product/vsrisk-cloud.

Here is a link for the information security risk management standards, ISO 27005:2018 and BS 7799-3:2017:

www.itgovernance.co.uk/shop/product/isoiec-27005-2018.

www.itgovernance.co.uk/shop/product/bs-7799-32017.

Who is vsRisk Cloud for?

Organisations of all sizes that need to conduct an information security risk assessment. These assessments are usually conducted by IT managers, IT risk managers, information security consultants/managers, compliance managers, DPOs, security analysts, CIO/CISOs or heads/directors of IT.

Appendix 1: vsRisk Cloud

What does vsRisk Cloud do?

Fully aligned with ISO 27001, vsRisk Cloud helps you deliver fast, accurate and hassle-free information risk assessments. It eliminates the need to use spreadsheets, which are prone to user input errors and can be difficult to set up and maintain, and enables you to produce consistent, robust and reliable risk assessments year after year. vsRisk Cloud allows users to work from anywhere provided they have an Internet connection and a compatible browser.

Fast and easy to use

You can identify risks by selecting assets, threats and vulnerabilities, and applying controls to reduce the risk to an acceptable level. The subscription includes five administrator/contributor users, which means that multiple people can work on a risk assessment at once. There is no limit to the number of read-only users.

Geared for repeatability

Repeat your risk assessments with ease. Because vsRisk Cloud doesn't rely on spreadsheets, which can easily become corrupted or unwieldy, you can conduct your risk assessment using exactly the same parameters as before.

Aligned with ISO 27001

vsRisk Cloud meets ISO 27001's requirements for consistent, valid and comparable results. The software includes control sets from ISO 27001:2005, ISO 27001:2013, ISO 27032:2012, NIST SP 800-53, CSA CCM v3, PCI DSS v3.2.1 and Cyber Essentials.

Appendix 1: vsRisk Cloud

Streamlined and accurate

vsRisk Cloud takes human error out of the equation. The 'risk assessment wizard' walks users through each step of identifying, evaluating and responding to an asset-based risk assessment to provide consistent, valid and comparable results. Users can also choose to adopt scenario-based assessments.

Generate auditable reports

vsRisk Cloud translates your risk assessment into the SoA and a risk treatment plan to help you meet ISO 27001's documentation requirements.

Integrates with other Vigilant Software products

vsRisk Cloud integrates with Compliance Manager and the Data Flow Mapping Tool, giving you full visibility of your compliance against a number of national and international laws around information security.

APPENDIX 2: ISO 27001 IMPLEMENTATION RESOURCES

Information and advice
www.itgovernance.co.uk/iso27001

Certification bodies and other organisations
www.itgovernance.co.uk/web_links

vsRisk
www.vigilantsoftware.co.uk

ISO 27001 ISMS Documentation Toolkit
www.itgovernance.co.uk/shop/product/iso-27001-iso27001-isms-documentation-toolkit

Information security standards ISO 27001, ISO 27002, ISO 27005 and BS 7799-3
www.itgovernance.co.uk/standards

ISO 27001 consultancy
www.itgovernance.co.uk/iso27001_consultancy

ISO 27001 training courses
www.itgovernance.co.uk/shop/category/iso-27001-training-courses

ISO 27001 books and pocket guides from ITGP
Application Security in the ISO 27001:2013 Environment
www.itgovernance.co.uk/shop/product/application-security-in-the-iso-27001-2013-environment-second-edition

Appendix 2: ISO 27001 implementation resources

Information Security Breaches: Avoidance and Treatment based on ISO27001
www.itgovernance.co.uk/shop/product/information-security-breaches-avoidance-and-treatment-based-on-iso27001-second-edition

ISO27001 in a Windows® Environment
www.itgovernance.co.uk/shop/product/iso27001-in-a-windows-environment-third-edition

ISO27001/ISO27002: A Pocket Guide
www.itgovernance.co.uk/shop/product/iso27001iso27002-a-pocket-guide-second-edition

Nine Steps to Success: An ISO27001 Implementation Overview
www.itgovernance.co.uk/shop/product/nine-steps-to-success-an-iso-27001-implementation-overview-third-edition

The Case for ISO 27001:2013
www.itgovernance.co.uk/shop/product/the-case-for-iso-27001-2013-second-edition

APPENDIX 3: BOOKS BY THE SAME AUTHORS

IT Governance - An International Guide to Data Security and ISO27001/ISO27002, Seventh Edition, Alan Calder and Steve G Watkins (published by Kogan Page, 2019)
www.itgovernance.co.uk/shop/product/it-governance-an-international-guide-to-data-security-and-iso27001iso27002-seventh-edition

The Case for ISO 27001:2013, Alan Calder (published by ITGP, 2013)
www.itgovernance.co.uk/shop/product/the-case-for-iso-27001-2013-second-edition

Nine Steps to Success: An ISO 27001 Implementation Overview, Third edition, Alan Calder (published by ITGP, 2016)
www.itgovernance.co.uk/shop/product/nine-steps-to-success-an-iso-27001-implementation-overview-third-edition

Selling Information Security to the Board - A Primer, Alan Calder (published by ITGP, 2016)
www.itgovernance.co.uk/shop/product/selling-information-security-to-the-board-a-primer

NIST Cybersecurity Framework - A pocket guide, Alan Calder (published by ITGP, 2018)
www.itgovernance.co.uk/shop/product/nist-cybersecurity-framework-a-pocket-guide

Appendix 3: Books by the same authors

Network and Information Systems (NIS) Regulations - A pocket guide for digital service providers, Alan Calder (published by ITGP, 2018)
www.itgovernance.co.uk/shop/product/network-and-information-system-nis-regulations-a-pocket-guide-for-digital-service-providers

Network and Information System (NIS) Regulations - A pocket guide for operators of essential services, Alan Calder (published by ITGP, 2018)
www.itgovernance.co.uk/shop/product/network-and-information-system-nis-regulations-a-pocket-guide-for-operators-of-essential-services

ISO27001/ISO27002: A Pocket Guide, Alan Calder (published by ITGP, 2013)
www.itgovernance.co.uk/shop/product/iso27001iso27002-a-pocket-guide-second-edition

EU GDPR: A pocket guide, Second edition, Alan Calder (published by ITGP, 2018)
www.itgovernance.co.uk/shop/product/eu-gdpr-a-pocket-guide-second-edition

Cyber Essentials: A pocket guide, Alan Calder (published by ITGP, 2014)
www.itgovernance.co.uk/shop/product/cyber-essentials-a-pocket-guide

Appendix 3: Books by the same authors

*An Introduction to Information Security and
ISO27001:2013 - A Pocket Guide,* Steve Watkins
(published by ITGP, 2013)
www.itgovernance.co.uk/shop/product/an-introduction-to-information-security-and-iso-27001-2013-a-pocket-guide-second-edition

*ISO27001 (2013) Assessments Without Tears: A Pocket
Guide, Second Edition,* Steve G Watkins (published by
ITGP, 2013)
www.itgovernance.co.uk/shop/product/iso27001-2013-assessments-without-tears-a-pocket-guide-second-edition

ISO 9001:2015 A pocket guide, Steve Watkins and Nick
Orchiston (published by ITGP, 2016)
www.itgovernance.co.uk/shop/product/iso-9001-2015-a-pocket-guide

FURTHER READING

IT Governance Publishing (ITGP) is the world's leading publisher for governance and compliance. Our industry-leading pocket guides, books, training resources and toolkits are written by real-world practitioners and thought leaders. They are used globally by audiences of all levels, from students to C-suite executives.

Our high-quality publications cover all IT governance, risk and compliance frameworks and are available in a range of formats. This ensures our customers can access the information they need in the way they need it.

Our other publications about information security include:

- *Information Security A Practical Guide* by Tom Mooney, *www.itgovernancepublishing.co.uk/product/information-security-a-practical-guide*
- *Cyberwar, Cyberterror, Cybercrime & Cyberactivism* by Julie Mehan, *www.itgovernancepublishing.co.uk/product/cyberwar-cyberterror-cybercrime-cyberactivism-2nd-edition*
- *The Psychology of Information Security* by Leron Zinatullin, *www.itgovernancepublishing.co.uk/product/the-psychology-of-information-security*

For more information on ITGP and branded publishing services, and to view our full list of publications, please visit www.itgovernancepublishing.co.uk.

To receive regular updates from ITGP, including information on new publications in your area(s) of interest, sign up for our newsletter at *www.itgovernancepublishing.co.uk/topic/newsletter*.

Branded publishing

Through our branded publishing service, you can customise ITGP publications with your company's branding.

Find out more at *www.itgovernancepublishing.co.uk/topic/branded-publishing-services.*

Related services

ITGP is part of GRC International Group, which offers a comprehensive range of complementary products and services to help organisations meet their objectives.

For a full range of resources on information security visit *www.itgovernance.co.uk/infosec*

Training services

The IT Governance training programme is built on our extensive practical experience designing and implementing management systems based on ISO standards, best practice and regulations.

Our courses help attendees develop practical skills and comply with contractual and regulatory requirements. They also support career development via recognised qualifications.

Learn more about our training courses in information security and view the full course catalogue at *www.itgovernance.co.uk/training*

Professional services and consultancy

We are a leading global consultancy of IT governance, risk management and compliance solutions. We advise businesses around the world on their most critical issues and present cost-saving and risk-reducing solutions based on international best practice and frameworks.

We offer a wide range of delivery methods to suit all budgets, timescales and preferred project approaches.

Find out how our consultancy services can help your organisation at *www.itgovernance.co.uk/consulting.*

Further reading

Industry news

Want to stay up to date with the latest developments and resources in the IT governance and compliance market? Subscribe to our Weekly Round-up newsletter and we will send you mobile-friendly emails with fresh news and features about your preferred areas of interest, as well as unmissable offers and free resources to help you successfully start your project:
www.itgovernance.co.uk/weekly-round-up.